What Others Are Saying About This Book

"I used Dragon to draft *Write & Grow Rich*. It made the hardest part of book writing quick, easy, and fun. Newman's *Guide* gives the inside story on making this software work in the best way possible."

— Dan Poynter, author of *The Self-Publishing Manual* and *Write & Grow Rich*

"I had used NaturallySpeaking for more than a year before finding this book. I wish I'd found it sooner! Any one of the tips on automating work easily justifies the cover price."

— Harris Lilienfeld, M.D. Delaware Valley Pediatric Associates, P.A.

"Speech software can be an important tool in recovering from a computer-related repetitive strain injury, if you have patience and appropriate guidance. This clear, practical book, written by an expert user who himself recovered from RSI, provides that guidance."

— Joan Lichterman, Founder East Bay RSI Support Group, one of the first U.S. support groups for people with repetitive strain injuries

"The information in this book has been vital to making speech software productive in my practice. My transcription bills have gone down sixty percent!"

— Donald Goldmacher, M.D. PsychComp Associates

THE
Dragon
NaturallySpeaking™
GUIDE

Speech Recognition
Made Fast and Simple

Second Edition

Dan Newman

Waveside Publishing
Berkeley, California

The Dragon NaturallySpeaking Guide: Speech Recognition Made Fast and Simple
Dan Newman

Waveside Publishing
2039 Shattuck Ave. Ste. 500, Berkeley, CA 94704

Cover design: Pawlak Design
Cover illustration: Barbara MacDonald
Author photograph: Lisa Marie Hadley

9 8 7 6 5 4 3 2 1

Printed on recycled paper

Publisher's Cataloging-in-Publication

Newman, Dan, (Dan G.)
   The Dragon NaturallySpeaking guide : speech
recognition made fast and simple /
Dan Newman.
         -- 2nd ed.
         p. cm.
         Dragon naturally speaking guide
         Includes index.
         LCCN: 99-91052
         ISBN: 0-9670389-7-9

   1. Automatic speech recognition. 2. Natural
language processing (Computer science) 3. Speech
processing systems. 4. Human-computer
interaction. 5. DRAGON (Computer system) I.
Title. II. Title: Dragon naturally speaking guide

TK7882.S65N49 2000   006.4'54

Foreword

James K. Baker, Ph.D.
Co-Founder, Dragon Systems, Inc.

Dragon NaturallySpeaking represents a long-term goal and milestone in speech recognition technology. When I joined speech recognition research in the early 1970s, mainframe computers would take up to an hour to recognize a single sentence from a restricted set of possibilities. The tasks we worked on were simplistic by today's standards, and the techniques we used look as pitiful compared to today's technology as do the computers on which we worked.

We looked beyond these limitations, however, to a very ambitious goal: recognition of unrestricted, large vocabulary, natural, continuous speech. This inspiring goal was the long-term milestone for myself and other people who began working on speech recognition technology in that era. We knew that achieving this goal would take a long time, but we believed we'd eventually succeed. Today, Dragon NaturallySpeaking can type as fast as you can speak, and you can say practically anything on any topic, speaking naturally and continuously.

Although for some speech researchers Dragon Naturally-Speaking represents the successful completion of a long journey, in another sense it is only the first step in an even bigger journey. As the "Natural Speech Company™," Dragon Systems is committed to providing speech as a natural interface between people and the machines and appliances they use. We continue to invest heavily in research and development to shorten enrollment time, support a wider choice of microphones, and allow more natural speaking styles.

We have worked hard to make Dragon NaturallySpeaking simple and easy to use. However, today's technology still has limitations. We cannot do everything you see on *Star Trek*. (After all, we still have another 200 years of research to do before the 23rd century!) Dragon NaturallySpeaking is optimized to a particular task—creating written text by voice. Unlike the *Star Trek* computer, it does not try to understand casual conversational speech and execute appropriate commands embedded within the conversation. It requires a careful speaking style that is only natural in the context of purposefully dictating a written document. You, the user, must be aware that you are talking to a computer and know how to work around its limitations. If you are not already used to composing by dictation, you will need to learn a new style of writing. If you are used to dictation, you will need to learn how much more you can do with a speech recognition computer than with a passive recorder. In any case, being proficient will require education and practice.

The Dragon NaturallySpeaking Guide fills the need for education. It will help users, new and experienced alike, learn how to write by voice and achieve optimum accuracy. From his years as a vendor and trainer of our product, author Dan Newman has learned hundreds of tips and tricks that without a guide you could learn only through long experience.

Then there's practice. Dan emphasizes the need for practice to build proficiency. Even if you had a secretary who could type everything you said as fast as you could say it, you would need practice to get used to the change in writing style. The computer, of course, imposes additional restrictions, which this book will help you learn and overcome. *The Dragon NaturallySpeaking Guide* will help you get up and running quickly so you can start practicing right away—and use the computer more productively, efficiently, and healthfully.

Acknowledgements

The many people who helped create this book include a talented team of readers, testers, and peer reviewers. Thanks to Bob Cowart, Don Goldmacher, Meredith Leslie, Dede Leydorf, Joan Lichterman, Michael Newman, Rochelle Newman, Dan Poynter, Deidre Rogers, Jeff Wolinsky, and Mark Zoeckler for their many useful suggestions. Special thanks to speech recognition experts Teresa Allen, Renee Griffith, and Mark Pearson for their reviews and feedback.

My deep appreciation goes to the staff of Dragon Systems for their support on this project. I'm especially indebted to Renata Aylward, Jim Baker, Jeff Foley, Carole Gunst, Valerie Matthews, Patrick Quinn, and Alexandra Trudo for their enthusiasm, assistance, and technical reviews.

My expert editor, Kristin Barendsen, has my sincere thanks for her assistance at every stage of creating this book, from helping to develop the initial outline to making detailed edits in the final text. Kristin, a Dragon software user herself, maintains an informative Web site about editing at www.barenedit.com.

Speech recognition is a new frontier in computing, and using it successfully requires a pioneer attitude. My greatest thanks go to the many speech recognition users my staff and I have had the opportunity to work with and train over the past four years. Their ingenuity and determination has created a richer book for all of us to learn from and enjoy.

Overview

Contents

6. Editing and Formatting 49

7. Web Surfing, Word, and WordPerfect 61

8. Numbers, Punctuation, and Capitalization 73

9. Hands-Free Computing 85

12. Workflow 131

13. Speaking and Dictating 145

14. Improving Performance 155

15. Healthy Computing............................ 179

16. Using the Dragon NaturallyMobile Recorder 187

17. Using Other Recorders............................ 195

21. Troubleshooting 239

Index 263

"Speech is not just the future of Windows, but the future of computing itself."

—*Microsoft Chairman Bill Gates*
in BUSINESS WEEK, *2-23-98*

Speech Recognition— The Next Revolution

Do you ever wish you could just talk to your computer?

To dictate a letter by voice rather than bang away at the keyboard with your hands?

To print a page simply by saying "print page 3?"

This one-time science fiction is now reality. In the summer of 1997, Dragon Systems made history by shipping Dragon NaturallySpeaking, the first software program that allows natural, rapid dictation to a PC.

This amazing program can transcribe your speech almost as quickly as you can talk. Freed from typing, you can sit back, relax, and dictate letters, memos, and e-mail. It's an easy, natural way to write. This book, in fact, was written by voice.

Fast, accurate speech recognition is a major breakthrough in computing. It will make computer use easier and more widespread. Many people who are turned off by the idea of interacting with computers are thrilled and intrigued when they first see a computer recognize spoken words. In future years, speech recognition might even replace the keyboard, as schoolchildren learn to dictate instead of type.

Why Work by Voice?

Dictation Is Fast and Natural

Doctors, attorneys, and others who compose text daily have long known that dictation is a fast, efficient way to write. Writing by voice lets you get your thoughts on paper quickly—faster even than expert typists.

Typing a transcript from tape is laborious and time-consuming, and not everyone can afford to hire a typist. For most people, the cost of writing by voice has been prohibitive.

Until NaturallySpeaking. Now, anyone with a PC can work the way only a fortunate few could before. Used well, the software acts as your own personal secretary, with 24-hour availability and virtually instant transcription. NaturallySpeaking can type what you say at 150 words per minute—if indeed you can speak that quickly.

Learning to compose out loud is an investment in your lifetime productivity. The sooner you start working by voice, the sooner you'll reap the benefits of improved speed and ease. If you already dictate into a tape recorder, you'll find that voice software makes writing even easier because the words you say appear immediately on screen.

Typing Can Hurt

Many people find using a keyboard difficult. Some people type slowly or never learn to type at all. Some have hand injuries or other disabilities that make typing difficult or impossible. Speech recognition is the keyboard alternative. If you can't type, or just don't want to, you can talk instead. With this software, you can do almost anything by voice that you can do with keyboard or mouse.

Typing can even cause or exacerbate damage to muscles, tendons, and nerves. Sitting in a static posture for hours with arms raised and fingers flying puts an unnatural load on the muscles of the upper back and arms. Almost everyone feels discomfort and stiffness while typing, and an alarming number of people are developing a painful condition called repetitive strain injury (RSI).

The problem is epidemic. Repetitive injuries are growing far more rapidly than other work-related problems. Many people with RSI become partially disabled, unable to use their arms normally and certainly unable to type. According to the U.S. Department of Labor Statistics, repetitive injuries resulted in the longest median absences from work of any frequent type of work-related injury. Speech recognition software can help people with RSI remain productive and employed and might even help prevent these injuries.

Even if you've never felt a twinge from the keyboard, speech is still a more comfortable way to work. You can sit, stand, move, and even stretch while dictating.

About This Book

Why Read This Book?

You already know how to speak—so why would you need a book to use NaturallySpeaking? For starters, the program isn't perfect. It guesses what you said, and often guesses wrong. There are many obstacles to reaching optimum accuracy, and overcoming these obstacles can be difficult without guidance. This book aims to help smooth out the frustrations, making writing by voice easy and fun.

First, to learn NaturallySpeaking, you'll have to learn a new way of interacting with the computer. You will give it auditory rather than keyboard commands, and train it to recognize your voice and vocabulary.

You'll also need to develop skill in composing out loud. If you're used to composing on paper or by typing, this will take practice. And figuring out how to use the software's advanced commands and correction features is not always obvious.

This book aims to make speech recognition practical for you. It guides you through getting started with the software, training the computer to recognize your voice, and learning how to get the computer to do what you want. It helps you choose a dictation style, create time-saving shortcuts to speed your work, and achieve greater speed and accuracy. Whether you're new to speech recognition or an experienced NaturallySpeaking user, this book will save you time and effort and make your work easier.

As founder of the speech recognition consulting firm Say I Can, I've had the pleasure of helping hundreds of clients use this technology successfully. My clients are excited by the software's potential and motivated to make it work well. They also have a high need for assistance. This book summarizes thousands of hours of dictation experience and problem-solving. I hope you'll find it clear, positive, and effective in helping you harness Dragon NaturallySpeaking's power.

Versions Covered

The information in this book is useful for all versions of NaturallySpeaking that start with 4, such as 4.0. NaturallySpeaking version 4 comes in several different editions, such as Standard, Preferred and Professional. Some features described in this book are not found in every edition, but most of the text will be useful to every NaturallySpeaking user.

If you have an earlier version of NaturallySpeaking, almost all of this book will still be useful to you. Using previous versions of the software is very similar to using version 4.

Assumptions

This guide assumes that you're already familiar with Windows 98, 95, or NT and with how to use your word processor and other applications.

Where to Start

If you're new to NaturallySpeaking, it's best to read the chapters in order. If you are already using NaturallySpeaking, start with Chapter 13, "Speaking and Dictating," and then read Chapter 14,

"Improving Performance." Next, browse Chapters 3 to 11 for a review of program commands. Read the other chapters for reference as you desire.

System Requirements

The minimum system requirements for NaturallySpeaking vary depending on the version of the software, and they're printed on the box and in the user manual. Minimum requirements, however, are just that. To use the software productively you'll need more memory and processor speed.

Minimum for Acceptable Performance

- Pentium (or equivalent) 200-MHz processor
- 64 MB of RAM
- sound card
- microphone

Best System

- fastest processor available
- 128 MB or more of RAM
- sound card with very clear signal (see "Sound Cards" below)
- high-quality microphone (see "Microphones" below)

The minimum processor speed—how many calculations the computer can do in a second—is 200-MHz. A higher number is better. RAM, the computer's active memory, determines how many programs can be running at the same time. Again, a higher number is better. Hard disk space is not an issue, as virtually all modern computers have at least the 200 MB of free hard disk space that NaturallySpeaking requires.

If you already have a computer, does it meet the minimum for acceptable performance?

- If it's less than the minimum, you'll probably be unhappy with the software's accuracy and responsiveness unless you upgrade your computer.
- If it's the minimum or better, load the software and try it. You can choose to upgrade your system at any time.

Almost any new computer you buy will be acceptable for NaturallySpeaking use. For best performance, choose a computer with 128 MB of RAM. More RAM is fine too, though it won't affect NaturallySpeaking performance. Buy the fastest processor that meets your budget—at least 400 MHz—and a good sound card.

Sound Cards

A sound card is a circuit board that allows the computer to play sound through speakers and to receive sound through a microphone. Before the advent of speech recognition software, users only cared whether the computer could play sound. Sound card makers focused on improving playback quality for music and games.

Speech recognition uses the other half of the sound card— the listening half. As you speak, your voice generates electrical impulses in the microphone. The sound card converts these impulses into numbers that NaturallySpeaking can analyze. Good sound cards faithfully measure the electrical changes your voice generates. Bad sound cards introduce static and interference, making it difficult or impossible for Naturally-Speaking to accurately determine what you said.

Most sound cards work fine for speech recognition. However, be sure to avoid "integrated" sound systems. In these systems, the sound circuitry is built in as part of the motherboard, the main computer circuit board. While this saves money for computer manufacturers, the sound wiring is physically closer to other circuitry and thus more likely to allow electrical interference to degrade the quality of the speech signal. If the system you buy has an integrated sound card and it gives poor results, you can still install a regular (nonintegrated) card and disable the integrated one.

Users report excellent results with two popular sound cards, the SoundBlaster 64 AWE and the Turtle Beach MultiSound Fiji Pro series. Many other cards also work well. Dragon Systems regularly tests sound cards and posts the results on their Web site, www.dragonsys.com. You should be able to get one of these cards included with your computer no matter where you purchase it. Like extra memory, the card you want will probably not be included in advertised computer packages. You need to ask to add these options to your system. Any computer vendor will be happy to oblige. If you're adding a sound card to a system that has integrated sound, ask the computer vendor to disable the integrated sound circuitry when assembling your system.

Laptops and Sound

Using speech recognition successfully on a laptop computer requires careful attention to the laptop model purchased. Many laptops are susceptible to electrical interference in sound recording, and they have built-in sound circuitry that cannot be changed. The sound circuitry is tightly packed among the rest of the laptop's wiring, making static and degradation of sound quality more common than with desktop computers. In addition, laptops occasionally pick up interference from a building's electrical wiring, giving them good sound quality running on battery power but poor results when plugged into the wall.

Some laptops work well for speech recognition while others work poorly. Dragon Systems evaluates laptops to ensure that they perform well with speech recognition, and test results are listed on their site at www.dragonsys.com. For best results, buy a laptop from a source familiar with speech recognition, or find one with a satisfaction guarantee or trial period to make sure the laptop works for your needs.

If your laptop does not give satisfactory sound quality from its built-in sound hardware, try a USB microphone. USB microphones use circuitry built-in to the microphone to process your voice signal before sending it to the computer.

Microphones

As of this writing, NaturallySpeaking Professional, Medical, and Legal editions include an excellent microphone, the VXI Parrott-10. This microphone provides a high-quality, high-level speech signal. The mic is also comfortable and easy to adjust.

Less expensive versions of NaturallySpeaking include a different microphone that, for most people, provides less optimal results with the software. Dictate with the microphone included with your software and see how it works. For most users, purchasing a better microphone will noticeably improve accuracy at a relatively low cost.

A new kind of microphone available is called USB (which stands for "Universal Serial Bus"). These microphones use circuitry built-in to the microphone to process your voice signal before sending it to the computer, bypassing the sound card. You'll still want a sound card for your computer so you can play sounds and music, but you won't need to worry about getting the best and most expensive model.

Many kinds of microphones are available, including hand-held and wireless models. See Chapter 20 for descriptions of common microphone models and manufacturer contact information.

2

Getting Started

If you haven't yet set up NaturallySpeaking, this chapter will guide you through each step of the process, from plugging in and positioning the microphone to training the computer to recognize your voice. Before you begin, restart your computer and turn off any active applications, including antivirus programs.

Plug in the Microphone and Speakers

Microphone

Find the mic plug at the end of the wire attached to the microphone. If the wire ends in just one plug, that's the mic plug. If the wire ends in two plugs, one is the mic plug and the other is for the speaker in the microphone's earpiece. Check the instructions included with your mic to figure out which is which. The mic plug sometimes has a small picture of a microphone imprinted in the plastic base of the plug. If the two jacks are different colors, the brightly colored one is usually the mic.

Next, find the mic jack in the sound card in your computer. On desktop computers, this small, round opening is almost always on the back of your computer. There will be one, two, or three similar-sized jacks next to it (all are part of your computer's sound hardware). Each jack should be labeled with words (MIC, LINE IN, SPKR) or pictures. Choose the jack with the word MIC or the picture of a microphone. The labels can be difficult to spot. They may be engraved into the metal plate the jacks are set into or imprinted on the plastic case of the computer.

On laptops, the mic jack may be on the side or front instead of the back of the computer.

Speakers

If you hear chimes or other sounds when Windows starts up, your speakers are already plugged in correctly. If Windows is silent, find the sound card jack labeled SPKR (or imprinted with a picture of a speaker), and plug in the speakers. This step is not necessary for laptops, which have internal speakers.

If your microphone has a speaker plug, you can listen to the computer's sound through the earphone on your headset mic. Beeps in the ear can be annoying, though, and most people do not use the microphone speaker plug. Just leave it unplugged.

Install NaturallySpeaking Software

Insert the NaturallySpeaking disk in the CD-ROM drive. In most cases the installation program will start automatically. Follow the on-screen instructions. If this does not work on your system, refer to the installation instructions included with the software.

If you are upgrading from an earlier version of NaturallySpeaking, version 4 will automatically upgrade your existing speech files. It's better to start from scratch, though, with a new user and new enrollment, as this is the only way to take advantage of all the accuracy improvements in version 4.

Multiple People on One Computer

Any number of people can use one copy of NaturallySpeaking on the same computer. The software keeps track of each person's pronunciations and custom words in separate "user files." When you start the program, NaturallySpeaking asks which user file it should work with this session.

If someone else has already set up NaturallySpeaking for their voice on your computer, you need to tell the program to create a new user file for you. To do this, start NaturallySpeaking, opening one of the existing user's voice files. Choose New from the User menu in NaturallySpeaking. Click Next to exit the welcome screen and continue with the instructions below.

After installation completes, a welcome screen will appear. Click Next, and NaturallySpeaking will ask you to choose a user name (Figure 2-1). Type your name. NaturallySpeaking picks the best speech model and vocabulary settings automatically.

If you have the Medical or Legal Edition of NaturallySpeaking, see the caption to Figure 2-1 for special instructions. If you are under 15 or have an unusually high voice, see the sidebar below, "Student Speech Models."

Student Speech Models

If you're between ages 9 and 15, you'll get the best accuracy by selecting a particular speech model and vocabulary called "Student." The Student speech model is specially tuned to recognize voices in that age range, and the Student vocabulary contains more of the words that younger speakers tend to use.

From the "Create User" screen (Figure 2-1), choose the Student version of whatever speech model the computer recommends. For example, if the computer recommends "BestMatch Model," as in Figure 2-1, change this to "Student BestMatch Model."

Select the proper vocabulary similarly—change the Vocabulary setting to the Student version of the vocabulary NaturallySpeaking has recommended. If the computer recommends "US General English - Bestmatch," change it to "Student General English - Bestmatch."

Figure 2-1
Type your name and
click Next.

For Medical and
Legal Editions,
select the proper
vocabulary before
pressing Next.
Change the "General
English" option to
the Medical or Legal
option in the
Vocabulary field.

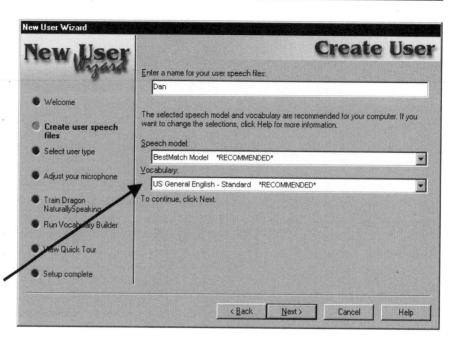

After you've entered your name, click Next. The next screen
asks whether you'll be dictating directly to the computer or into
a portable recorder. Choose "Directly to the computer" (Figure 2-
2) and click Next.

Figure 2-2
Choose "Directly to
the computer" and
click Next.

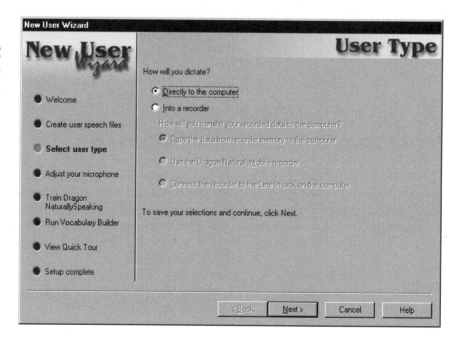

Click Next again for the screen titled "Choose your input device" (Figure 2-3). Select the type of microphone you're using and click Next. For best results, use a headset mic, like the one included with your software. To properly position your microphone, follow the instructions here.

Figure 2-3
Select your
microphone type
and click Next.

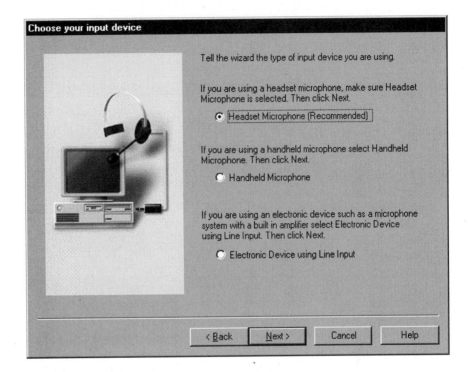

Position the Microphone

Put the microphone on your head so that the headband goes across the top of your head. Adjust the headband so that it is comfortable and feels like it will stay in place. For additional comfort, most mics can be adjusted so that the boom extends down from either the left ear or the right ear, as you prefer.

Figure 2-3
Parts of a headset
microphone.

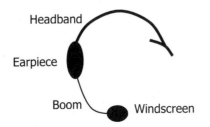

Next, bend or adjust the boom so that the foam windscreen, which shields the microphone element from excess noise, is near your mouth. Correct positioning is crucial for recognition accuracy. Start with the mic at the corner of your mouth, about a thumb's width away.

At the Corner of Your Mouth

If the mic is too close to the center of your mouth, it may pick up breathing sounds, which NaturallySpeaking often mistakes for "the," "a," or other small words. Move it closer to the corner.

The Right Distance Away

The windscreen should not touch your face, hair, or beard. The proper distance from your mouth is roughly between one-half and one inch—about the width of the thick part of your thumb.

Place your thumb between the mic and your mouth. One side of your thumb should be touching your mouth, the other should be just brushing the windscreen. Checking this distance with your thumb is a good way to get a feel for proper microphone positioning. While you work, the microphone may shift, degrading recognition accuracy. Giving a quick "thumb check" ensures that the mic is where it should be.

Pointing Toward Your Mouth

To pick up the best sound, the microphone element should be pointed toward your mouth. The microphone element, covered by the foam windscreen, is the electronic part that actually hears your voice. On most mics a small dot just outside the windscreen indicates the direction the microphone hears best. Be sure that dot is pointed toward your mouth. (On some mics you may need to partially remove the windscreen to find the dot. Other mics have a flat edge near the mic element rather than a dot—point the flat edge toward your mouth.)

Positioned Consistently

Consistent mic placement is absolutely vital for accurate speech recognition. Position the mic exactly the same way each time you use the software. If the mic drifts, your voice will sound different to the computer, and your text might come out garbled.

Audio Setup

After you choose your input device in Figure 2-3, Naturally-Speaking will display some tips on proper microphone placement. Click Next to begin audio setup, a two-part process that lets NaturallySpeaking adjust your computer's internal settings so that it can hear your voice most clearly. From the screen "Adjust your volume" (Figure 2-4), click the Start Adjusting button (Figure 2-4) and read the text that appears.

Figure 2-4
Click the Start Adjusting button, then read the text that appears.

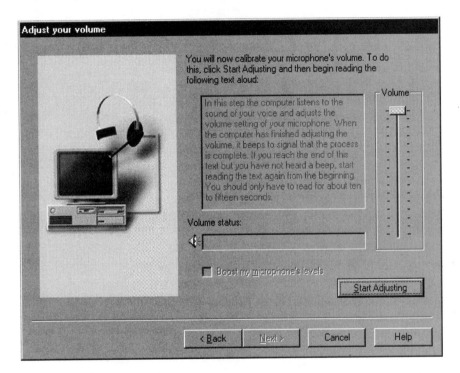

After NaturallySpeaking adjusts your volume setting, click Next for the screen "Check your audio quality" (Figure 2-5). Click the Start Quality Check button and read the on-screen text. As you read, the computer is evaluating your sound setup. After about a minute, NaturallySpeaking will display a "signal-to-noise" ratio, which indicates the clarity of your sound system. If NaturallySpeaking labels this measurement "ACCEPTABLE," you're ready to go on—click the Finish button to continue. If not, consult "Testing Your Sound System," page 240.

Figure 2-5
Click Start Quality
Check button, then
read the text that
appears.

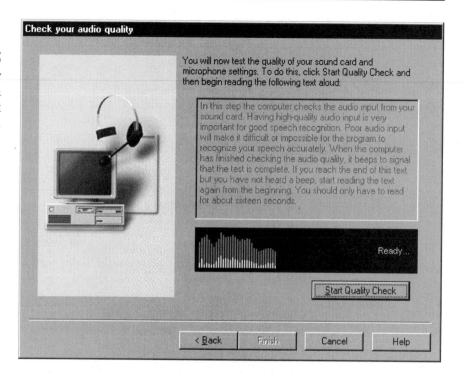

Figure 2-6
Click the Run
Training Program
button.

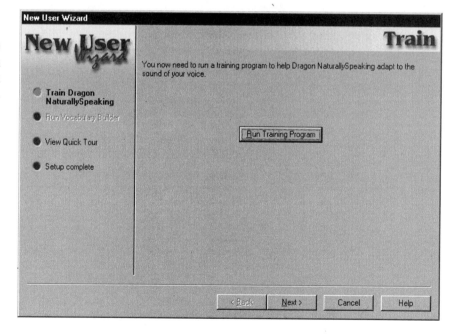

New User Enrollment

Follow the on-screen prompts to begin enrollment, the process of training NaturallySpeaking to recognize your voice (Figure 2-6). Have some drinking water at hand before you begin.

Enrollment takes place in two parts. The first part consists of reading a few paragraphs aloud and takes about two minutes (Figure 2-7).

Figure 2-7
Read this sentence without pausing. If the computer does not move to the next sentence, read it again. The yellow volume meter should change to green as you speak.

Volume Meter ——►

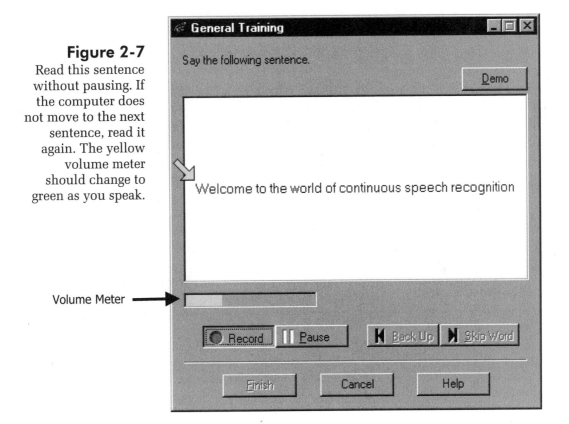

NaturallySpeaking will perform an initial calibration, adjusting a generic set of pronunciations to fit how you speak. Next, the software will ask you to choose a training text to read (Figure 2-8). Select the text you prefer to read and click Next.

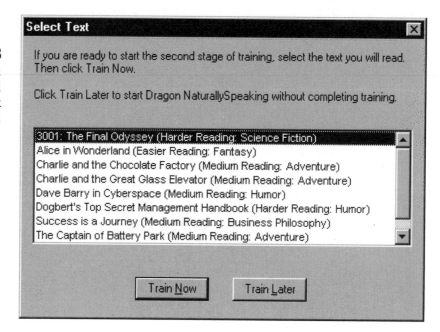

Figure 2-8
Select the text you prefer to read and click Train Now.

Now, fasten your seatbelt, because for the next few minutes you'll read passages that appear on-screen (Figure 2-9). Mercifully, you can take a break at any time by pressing the Pause button. Press Record to resume. You'll be reading for either five minutes or about thirty minutes, depending upon the processor speed of your computer.

As you speak, the words you say turn from blue to black, showing that NaturallySpeaking hears them. If you pause, a yellow arrow will show you where to begin speaking again. Occasionally you'll read a sentence or paragraph, but Naturally-Speaking will not advance and the yellow arrow will point to the start of what you already read. This indicates that something in the passage you read did not match what NaturallySpeaking expected to hear. Read the passage again, pausing after every sentence. If you cannot get past a particular word after saying it three times, click the Skip Word button to continue.

When you've read enough, a message will appear asking if you want to finish training or keep reading (Figure 2-10) Click Finish to adapt (create) your voice files. Depending on your computer, this will take from two minutes to a half hour or more. When adaptation is complete, follow the on-screen instructions to finish setting up your user. The NaturallySpeaking window

will appear, waiting for you to start talking. Congratulations—
you're ready to dictate!

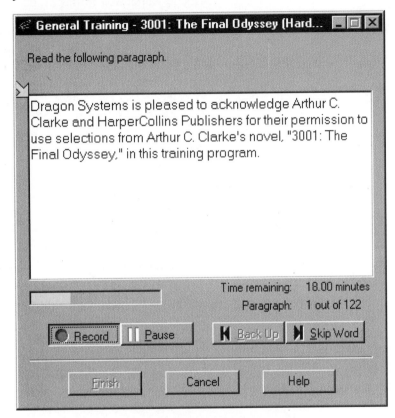

Figure 2-9
Read the passage
shown.

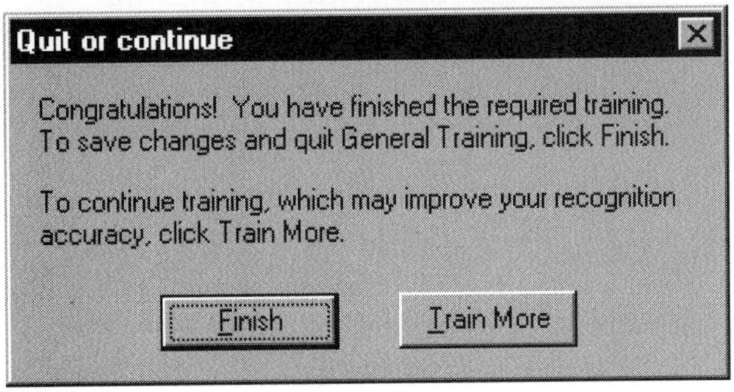

Figure 2-10
Click Finish to
complete initial
training.

Accents

NaturallySpeaking works well with a variety of accents. Train the computer by enrolling as usual. The program will usually adapt. You may have to repeat some words and phrases during training.

The program cannot adapt to every accent, however. If you must repeat almost everything you read during enrollment for the computer to move to the next phrase, NaturallySpeaking is having trouble adapting its pronunciation models to how you speak. The program probably will not be productive for you, as its accuracy will be too low to be useful. You might consider trying a different language version of NaturallySpeaking (though these don't allow English dictation), or Dragon Systems' older program, DragonDictate. While DragonDictate adapts well to almost any voice, it uses older technology that requires pausing between words. NaturallySpeaking is available in Spanish, Italian, German, French, U.K. English, and U.S. English. For information on where to purchase these products, see Chapter 20.

Enrollment Problems and Solutions

Symptom: Nothing changes on the screen as you speak, and the yellow volume bar stays yellow.

Cause: NaturallySpeaking is not hearing your voice.

Solution: Check that the mic is plugged in correctly. If the volume bar still does not move as you speak, run the Audio Setup Wizard again.

Symptom: The yellow volume bar changes to red as you talk.

Cause: The sound signal is too loud.

Solution: Run the Audio Setup wizard again. Also try moving the mic farther away from your mouth, or use a different mic.

Symptom: The volume bar changes to green as you speak (as it's supposed to), but NaturallySpeaking does not move on to the next sentence when you read "Welcome to the world of continuous speech recognition."

Causes and Solutions: Some users must say this sentence twice. Say the sentence again, without pausing. It is also possible that your voice does not match NaturallySpeaking's model closely enough for the program to continue. Pause quietly for five seconds, then say the sentence again, without pausing. Enunciate each word clearly.

3

The Basics

If you haven't yet dictated your first sentence, now's your chance. In this chapter, you'll learn basic techniques for dictating into the NaturallySpeaking window, moving text between applications, and speaking directly into other programs.

Throughout this book, NaturallySpeaking commands are capitalized (Scratch That, Delete Next 3 Words), as they are capitalized in the NaturallySpeaking documentation and as NaturallySpeaking displays them on screen.

The NaturallySpeaking Window

The NaturallySpeaking window (Figure 3-1) is a simple word processor. It works like WordPad, the bare-bones application that comes with Windows. The NaturallySpeaking window performs well for dictating simple documents, and it's a good tool to practice correcting errors by voice. After you dictate, you can print, save, or move your text to an e-mail program or other word processor.

Figure 3-1
The
NaturallySpeaking
window.

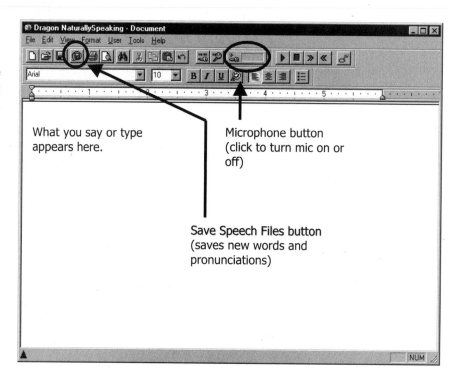

What you say or type
appears here.

Microphone button
(click to turn mic on or
off)

Save Speech Files button
(saves new words and
pronunciations)

Dictating Your First Sentence

Click the Microphone button to turn the microphone on. The button changes to show if the mic is off or on.

Off—the computer can't hear you.

On—the computer is listening. It will type whatever it hears.

Say "testing" to be sure the computer hears you. The word "testing," or maybe another word, will appear on screen.

Is There a Delay?

On many systems, there will be a 10- to 30-second delay before the computer acts on the first thing you say. This delay is most common on systems with less than 64 MB of memory. If nothing appears after 30 seconds, check that the microphone is turned on and try again.

Next, dictate a sentence about the weather. Or read this:
"I am now able to talk to my computer!"
(Say "exclamation point" for "!").

Did It Work?

If only one or two words appear, your microphone may be set up incorrectly or your sound settings may need to be changed. See page 240 for instructions on how to test your sound system.

If words did appear, but many are incorrect (not what you said), that's OK. NaturallySpeaking will improve the more you use it.

Go ahead and dictate whatever you like. Remember to say punctuation:

- ▶ , "comma"
- ▶ . "period"
- ▶ ! "exclamation point"
- ▶ ? "question mark"
- ▶ - "hyphen"

For a new paragraph, say "New Paragraph" run together as one word, with no pause after "new."

After dictating a paragraph or two, go back and correct the computer's mistakes with the keyboard and mouse. You'll learn to correct by voice in Chapter 5.

Key Tips for Dictating

- ▶ Pronounce each word clearly—even short words.
- ▶ Speak all punctuation ("comma," "period," and so on).
- ▶ Say commands without pausing between the words ("NewParagraph").
- ▶ Commands require a pause before and after the command ("Select Last 3 Words (pause) Bold That"). The pauses help NaturallySpeaking separate commands from words to be typed.

▶ Pretend you're talking to a person—speech with lively inflection tends to be processed more accurately than speech in a dull monotone. Put a friend's photo next to the computer to remind you. For more speaking tips, see Chapter 13.

▶ Looking at the screen while speaking can be distracting. Look away from the computer as you speak, or close your eyes.

▶ To maintain your line of thought, dictate a paragraph or two at a time. Then go back and correct, with what you said still in mind.

▶ Drink lots of water.

▶ Click Save Speech Files (Figure 3-1) at least once per computer session.

Turning the Microphone On and Off

Any of these three methods will switch the mic between on and off:

▶ Press the numeric "+" key on your keyboard. This key is at the far right of most keyboards. (It's not the plus key that is paired with the "=" sign.)

▶ Click on the Microphone button in the NaturallySpeaking window.

▶ Click on the small microphone picture in the bottom right corner of the screen, next to the clock:

Saying "Microphone Off" will also turn the microphone off. You cannot turn the microphone on by voice.

Whenever you're not using NaturallySpeaking, turn off the microphone. This prevents the computer from mistaking background noise for words and filling your screen with useless text.

Sleeping and Waking Up

Saying "Go To Sleep" without pausing will put NaturallySpeaking into sleep mode. The program still listens to your speech, but the only phrase it will respond to in this mode is "Wake Up," which turns the microphone all the way on.

When in sleep mode:

▶ The microphone button in the NaturallySpeaking window will show a dark gray volume bar (instead of yellow or green).
▶ The mic picture at the bottom corner of the screen will show "zzz" in light gray, just above the mic:

"Go to Sleep" can be useful for phone calls or other short interruptions. If you leave the computer, though, turn the mic all the way off, so that NaturallySpeaking does not hear "Wake Up" accidentally.

Practically speaking, most people find that using the "+" key is the simplest on/off method.

Printing, Saving, and Moving

Now that the words you said are on the computer's screen, you can print, save, copy, and paste them, just as if you had typed them.

Printing

From the File menu, use the mouse to choose Print. Or say "Click File," pause, and say "Click Print."

Saving

From the File menu, choose Save. Or say "Click File," pause, "Click Save." Your words can be saved as either text (.txt format) or rich text (.rtf format). Rich text is usually the best choice, since it preserves fonts, underlining, and other formatting. Your saved file may be opened in virtually any Windows word processor, including Word, WordPerfect, and WordPad.

Moving Text to Another Application

To copy your dictation to a word processor, e-mail program, or spreadsheet, you can use familiar menu or keyboard commands, or you can move the text by voice.

With Menu Commands

1. Select the text you want to copy.
2. From the Edit menu, choose Copy.
3. Switch to the other program.
4. Position the cursor where you want the new text to appear.
5. From the Edit menu, choose Paste.

By Keyboard

From the NaturallySpeaking window:

1. Press Ctrl+A (Select All).
2. Press Ctrl+C (Copy).
3. Press Alt+Tab (to change to a different program). Hold down Alt, and tap Tab repeatedly until the program you want appears. Then let go of the Alt key.
4. Press Ctrl+V (Paste).
5. Press Alt+Tab (to change back to NaturallySpeaking, if you wish).

By Voice

From the NaturallySpeaking window:

1. Say "Copy All to Clipboard" (like all commands, say this without pausing between the words)
2. Say "Switch to Next Window" (this will bring up the most recent program used before switching to the NaturallySpeaking window). Or, say "Switch to Previous Window."
3. Say "Paste That" (pastes the text wherever the cursor is).
4. Say "Switch to NatSpeak" (to change back to NaturallySpeaking, if you wish).

Dictating Into Other Programs

When you just want to send off a few quick e-mails, it's easier to dictate directly into the e-mail program than into the Naturally-Speaking window. You can dictate into many applications, including e-mail, spreadsheet, and word processing programs. First, start NaturallySpeaking, then switch to the program where you want your words to appear.

Next, click the mouse where you'd normally start typing, such as the message window in an e-mail program.

Turn the microphone on. (Press the "+" key on the keypad, or click the small microphone picture next to the clock at the bottom corner of the screen.) Now the words you say will appear in your e-mail program. See Chapter 7 for special instructions on dictating into Word and Word Perfect.

When the computer makes mistakes, edit them the traditional way for now—with keyboard and mouse. Chapters 5 and 6 describe how to edit text by voice.

Learning and Getting Help

Two resources that automatically install with NaturallySpeaking can help you learn the program better:

- ▶ "Quick Tour" movie clips demonstrate how to use common features.
- ▶ On-screen Help can be useful in learning and remembering what commands you can say.

Quick Tour

From the Help menu, choose Quick Tour. (You may need to insert the NaturallySpeaking CD-ROM.) The Quick Tour consists of short video clips demonstrating common spoken commands. View the Quick Tour now if you haven't already.

On-Screen Help

You can open Help in three ways:

- ▶ Say "Give Me Help"
- ▶ In the NaturallySpeaking window, press F1.

▶ In the NaturallySpeaking window, from the Help menu choose Help Topics.

The Help screen that appears is sometimes "context-sensitive," providing information relevant to the part of the program you're using. As with most computer programs, the on-screen Help is sometimes useful and sometimes not. You can print individual Help topics with the Print button in the Help window.

"What Can I Say?"

Asking "What Can I Say?" will bring up the on-screen Help section that lists available spoken commands. This information is also summarized in Chapters 5 through 9.

What's on the Screen

The NaturallySpeaking window includes many buttons and controls. This chapter explains how they work.

Button Bars

At the top of the NaturallySpeaking window are button bars that let you choose commands with a mouse click (Figure 4-1).

Figure 4-1
The three button bars and the ruler.

You can make each button bar and the ruler appear or disappear by choosing it from the View menu.

Format Bar

The Format bar works like it does in any word processor, as does the ruler below it.

Toolbar

On the Toolbar, ten buttons work as they do in any word processor:

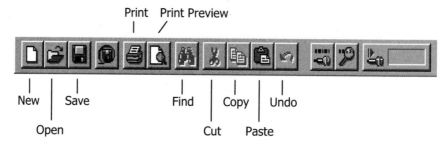

Four buttons are special to NaturallySpeaking:

Save Speech Files

Click this button to save the pronunciations and new words the computer has learned. As you use NaturallySpeaking and correct mistakes, the program adapts to your voice and becomes more accurate.

Your speech files contain a computer model of how your voice sounds, plus statistical information about what words you use most often. Save your speech files at the end of every session, so the computer remembers the mistakes you corrected and improves over time. You might not want to save your speech files if your voice is different than usual, such as when you have a cold, or if the computer is much less accurate than usual.

Saving your speech files is different than saving the text you wrote. If you want to save your document—the text—choose

Save from the File menu. In most cases, you'll save your document frequently as you write and save your speech files just once before shutting down the computer.

Train Words

If the computer consistently misrecognizes a word, you can use this button to teach the computer what you said. See page 175 for details.

Find New Words

With this button you can teach the computer a group of new words all at once. You probably won't use it often. See page 173 for instructions.

Microphone On/Off

When the mic is on, a colored bar shows the current sound level. Yellow indicates silence or speech that is too soft, green indicates proper speech level, and red indicates sound that is too loud to be processed.

Playback Bar

The first two buttons on the Playback bar control recorded speech playback. See "Play That Back" and "Stop Playback" below. The buttons with double-arrows speed up and slow down playback. The last button on the right opens the Correction window to teach the computer what you said (see Chapter 5).

Play That Back

Select a word, sentence, or paragraph, then click this button to hear a recording of what you said. A yellow arrow points to the text during playback to show you how the computer interpreted your words. This button is invaluable for editing when you don't remember what you said.

If you've edited your text or moved around in your document, this button often does not work—you'll see a red arrow instead of a yellow one, and hear nothing.

Stop Playback

Click this button to stop the recorded speech playback.

The Mic in the Taskbar

When NaturallySpeaking is running, one of three small graphics will appear next to the clock in the corner of the screen:

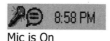 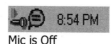 

Mic is On   Mic is Off   Mic is Sleeping

The microphone icon indicates whether the microphone is on or off. You can click on this picture to switch the mic on or off.

The bubble icon indicates that NaturallySpeaking is running, and that you can dictate into any program. If for some reason you wish to disable dictation into all programs other than NaturallySpeaking, click once on the bubble.

Results Box

The Results box is a small yellow window that appears as you dictate. It looks like this: business address

As you speak, the Results box displays the words that NaturallySpeaking thinks you said. These words change as the program considers different interpretations of your sounds. After NaturallySpeaking types the text into your document, the Results box shows what was typed.

A line at the bottom of the Results box changes color from yellow to green as you speak. This line is a volume meter that duplicates the microphone volume meter at the top of the NaturallySpeaking window.

You can move the Results box anywhere on the screen by dragging it with the mouse. You can also stop NaturallySpeaking in the middle of recognizing a phrase. To do this, click on the small red circle in the upper left corner of the Results box.

The Results box is useful in three ways. When you notice the volume meter change to green, you know the computer is actually hearing you. When you see the Results box fill with words, you know that NaturallySpeaking is processing what you say. And finally, after you finish a command or phrase, the Results box shows you what NaturallySpeaking thought you said. You can then determine whether NaturallySpeaking recognized your commands.

You can change the size of the Results box or fix it permanently in one place with the Options command on the Tools menu (see page 212).

5

Correcting Errors

You may have already noticed an axiom of NaturallySpeaking: the words the computer types are not always the words you said. "Erica" becomes "haircut," "sunny day" becomes "onion bay." NaturallySpeaking's mistakes can be at once frustrating and hilarious. But don't despair—as you correct its errors, the computer learns more about how you speak, and your accuracy improves. This chapter shows you how to begin. Chapter 6 covers making other kinds of changes to your text, such as fixing misspoken words, rewriting, and revising.

Two Kinds of Mistakes

Dictation errors come in two flavors: misspoken words and misrecognized words.

Misspoken

You stopped in the middle of a word, coughed, said "um," or otherwise said other than what you meant.

- ▶ You say: "I really want some uh new software."
- ▶ It types: "I really want some a new software."

To erase the last few words you said, say "Scratch That." You can say "Scratch That" repeatedly to keep erasing. For other ways to edit misspoken words, see the editing commands in Chapter 6.

Misrecognized

NaturallySpeaking types the wrong word.

- ▶ You say: "Computers can bring both joy and frustration."
- ▶ It types: "Computers can bring both joined frustration."

For a misrecognized word, teach the computer what you actually said by using the Correction window, described in "Teaching the Computer," page 38.

When Can You Teach the Computer?

In the NaturallySpeaking window, you can select any misrecognition in the whole document and teach the computer what you actually said. You can also do this in Microsoft Word and WordPerfect. These special programs are called "Select-and-Say" applications. Select-and-Say applications include Microsoft Word 97 and 2000, Microsoft Outlook 97 and 2000, Corel WordPerfect 8 and 9, WordPad, Notepad, Microsoft Chat versions 2.1 and 2.5, and GoldMine. (For special instructions on using Word and WordPerfect, see Chapter 7.)

In applications that are not Select-and-Say, you can still teach the computer to correct a misrecognition, but only if the misrecognition is in the last phrase you said. In these programs, you cannot select words and phrases by speaking them.

Use the NaturallySpeaking window for all dictating and correcting until you're thoroughly comfortable with the process. Then move on to dictating in other Select-and-Say programs.

Simple Corrections: Select and Redictate

Select a misrecognition by saying "Select" plus the words you want to correct. Then redictate your original words.

Here's an example of how this process works:

You say	The computer shows
Nothing exceeds like excess.	Nothing exceeds the excess.
Select the (to select the incorrect word)	Nothing exceeds **the** excess.
like (to redictate the correct word)	Nothing exceeds like excess.

When saying commands, including "Select...," pause before and after the command. Do not pause in the middle of the command. In the example above, say "(pause) Select the (pause)."

Redictating text that was misrecognized, as in this example, does not change your speech files. Your document is corrected, but NaturallySpeaking did not learn from its mistake.

The Selection Commands

These commands select text by voice.

Example	General form
Select the (where "the" is a misrecognized word	Select <text>
Select exceeds to excess (selects a range of words, from the first word to the second)	Select <text> to <text> Select <text> through <text>
Select Again (if the computer chooses the wrong occurrence of the word you said)	Select Again

When you say "Select Las Vegas" NaturallySpeaking searches backwards until it finds those words. You can change the search direction to forward (see page 217), but leaving it set as backwards is most practical.

How NaturallySpeaking Searches

- ▶ NaturallySpeaking searches backwards, starting at the cursor.
- ▶ The program searches only the text currently visible on the screen.
- ▶ If it doesn't find the word you said above the cursor, it will continue searching from the bottom of the screen.

Tips on Selecting

- ▶ Say "Select Again" if the computer highlights the right words but in the wrong place. This may happen if the words you're looking for occur more than once on the screen.
- ▶ If the word you want to select does occur more than once, try selecting two words instead of one. For example, say "Select the excess" if "Select the" is not specific enough.
- ▶ If the computer selects words other than what you said, try repeating "Select _____" again, just as you said it the first time. Often NaturallySpeaking will get it right the second time.

If you prefer, you can select text with the keyboard or mouse instead of with voice commands. Just click and drag across the text with the mouse (or use keyboard editing shortcuts, see page 52). Then redictate the correct text.

Teaching the Computer

I Said It Again, But It Still Comes Out Wrong

Often you'll redictate to try to fix a mistake, but the computer will generate another mistake. When this happens, it's time to teach the computer. Say "Correct That" to bring up a window where you tell the computer what you said. The computer learns from this and will be more likely to get your dictation right next time.

*Use "Correct That" only when the computer makes a mistake (when what you say is misrecognized). Do **not** use "Correct That" to fix mistakes **you** make, like mispronouncing a word or changing your mind in the middle of a sentence.*

The example below shows how to use NaturallySpeaking's Correction window. In this example, spelling is done by keyboard, the easiest way to learn. You can also spell by voice using the instructions later in this chapter.

You say	The computer shows
Nothing exceeds like excess.	Nothing exceeds the excess.
Select the (to select the incorrect word)	Nothing exceeds **the** excess.
like (to redictate the correct word—but NaturallySpeaking gets it wrong)	Nothing exceeds Mike excess.

Say "Correct That" (to open the Correction window). The computer shows:

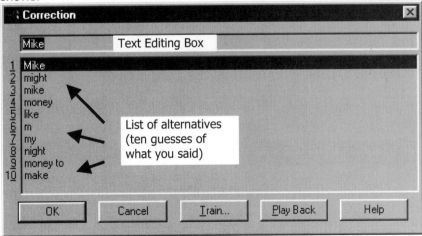

Type "like" and press Enter to teach the computer what you actually said. The Correction window disappears, your correction appears in the document, and Naturally-Speaking has learned your voice better.
    Nothing exceeds like excess.

Important Details, Options, and Alternate Methods

There are three ways to open the Correction window:

▶ Say "Correct That."
▶ Say "Spell That."
▶ Press the "-" (minus) key on the numeric keypad.

If text is selected, this text will appear in the Correction window. If no text is selected, NaturallySpeaking shows the words you said since your last pause.

Here's another way of putting it. When you say "Correct That," "That," according to the computer, is whatever text is selected at the moment. If nothing is selected, "That" refers to the last few words you dictated—everything since your last pause.

There's a fourth way to open the Correction window, too. You can say "Correct" plus the words you want to fix, and the Correction window will open with those words already in it. "Correct Alaska," for example, acts like saying these two commands: "Select Alaska," then "Correct That."

For most people, saying these two separate commands works more smoothly. By saying "Select" before "Correct," you can make sure NaturallySpeaking found the words you want to fix. Experiment to see which method is easiest for you.

Once the Correction window is open, enter the word or phrase you actually said through one of two ways:

▶ Type the word or phrase you said.
▶ Spell letter by letter ("t-h-e"). It's okay to run the letters together without pausing. For more details, see "Spelling in the Correction Window," below.

If the word or phrase you said appears among the ten options in the Correction window list, you don't need to enter the word letter by letter. Instead:

▶ Double-click on the correct word, or
▶ Say "Choose 3" to pick word or phrase 3 in the list. (Use a number from 1 to 10.) In the correction example above, the correct word, "like," is in position 5. Instead of typing "like," you could say "Choose 5."

Spelling in the Correction Window

To spell in the correction window, either say the letter ("a," "b," "c," etc.) or use the radio alphabet.

Radio Alphabet				
alpha	golf	Mike	Sierra	Yankee
bravo	hotel	November	tango	Zulu
Charlie	India	Oscar	uniform	
delta	Juliet	papa	Victor	
echo	kilo	Quebec	whiskey	
foxtrot	Lima	Romeo	x-ray	

You can say letters and radio alphabet words either run together or in a letter-by-letter staccato. Saying letters one after another, without pausing, is usually more accurate. Note that you can't dictate whole words in the Correction window.

Saying letters the normal way is easier to remember, but less accurate, than the radio alphabet. NaturallySpeaking has difficulty distinguishing between similar-sounding letters, like "g," "b," "c," "e," and "d." The radio alphabet is very accurate. These particular words were originally chosen to be easily distinguished from each other over poor radio connections.

When spelling in the Correction window, you can say the numbers 0 through 9. You can also say "Double" plus a letter to double it when you're spelling. "Balloon," for example, could be spelled "b-a-double-l-double-o-n."

Uppercase Letters

Say "Cap" plus the letter, without pausing. To spell "Vegas," for example, say "Cap-v-e-g-a-s" or "Cap-victor-echo-golf-alpha-sierra."

Punctuation

Pause before and after saying punctuation:

space-bar
period
question mark
exclamation point *or* exclamation mark

hyphen (-)	
dash (--) (a double hyphen)	
apostrophe	
apostrophe-ess ('s)	
slash	

For less common punctuation, see the punctuation table on page 77.

Special Characters

In the correction window, you can enter special characters by voice. Here are some of the most common special characters. You can only dictate a special character into your document once you've first entered it as a word in the Correction window (see page 80 for more detail on how to do this.)

To type	Say one of these
™	trademark
	trademark sign
©	copyright
	copyright sign
®	registered
	registered sign
	registered trademark
—	em dash
(nonbreaking space)	nonbreakable space
	unbreakable space
	no break space
°	degree
	degree sign
¼	quarter
	one quarter
½	half
	one half
^{1}	superscript 1
^{2}	superscript 2
	squared
^{3}	superscript 3
	cubed

You can dictate many other special characters too, including, all accented and international characters. For a full list of special characters and their names, search for "spelling characters" in NaturallySpeaking's online help (choose "Help Topics" from the NaturallySpeaking Help menu).

Start to Spell Early

You can start spelling before the Correction window appears. If the word you said is "like," say "Spell That l-i-k-e" without pausing. The Correction window will open with these letters already typed in it.

Recommendations

▶ Spelling by voice can be tedious and inaccurate. If there's one place in NaturallySpeaking where you'll want to type, this would be it.

▶ If you can't type or don't want to, use the radio alphabet. It's much more accurate than saying individual letters. Keep the alphabet by your computer for reference, then memorize it.

Voice Commands in the Correction Window

Use these commands to control the Correction window by voice:

Say "Choose 3" if alternative 3 in the Correction window is what you said. ("Choose 1" picks alternative 1, which is always the same as what's in the text editing box.)

Say "Select 3" if alternative 3 is *close* to what you said. The text is copied to the text editing box for you to change.

To click the on-screen buttons by voice, say "Click OK," "Click Cancel," "Click Train," "Click Play Back," or "Click Help."

To edit in the text editing box, say:

▶ "Backspace" to delete the previous character
▶ "Backspace 5" to delete the previous 5 characters (can say any number 2 to 20)
▶ "Press Home Key" or "Go to Top" to jump to start of text.
▶ "Press End Key" or "Go to Bottom" to jump to end of text.
▶ "Delete Next 4 Characters," "Delete Back 2 Words."

▶ More generally: "Delete (or) Select
<Next/Previous/Forward/Back> <1-20>
<Characters/Words>."

▶ "Select Line (pause) Cut That" to clear the whole text
editing box.

Note that "Scratch That" does not work in the Correction
window.

Keyboard Shortcuts in the Correction Window

Use these commands to control the Correction window by
keyboard:

Press Alt+3 if alternative 3 in the Correction window is what
you said. Press Alt+0 to pick alternative 10. (Alt+1 always picks
what's in the text editing box.)

Press Enter to hit the "OK" button and close the window. This
has the same effect as Alt+1.

Press Alt+P to play back the sound of what you said.

Accuracy Is Key

When you're using the Correction window, you're teaching the
computer by associating the sounds you made with particular
words on screen. It's important to make sure to teach the
computer correctly, or it will "mislearn" and its accuracy will
degrade.

▶ Click Play Back in the Correction window to hear what you
actually said. Be sure that the words you hear match what
you're entering in the Correction window.

▶ Check the text you enter in the Correction window to avoid
teaching the computer misspelled words.

▶ Don't use the Correction window to correct misspeaks,
such as coughs or incomplete words.

▶ Don't use the Correction window to edit your writing.

More Tips on the Correction Window

As you type or spell, the options in the correction list will change to match the first few letters you typed. Often it's necessary to type or spell only a few characters, then choose the right words from the correction list.

The Train button lets you pronounce your word or phrase again to teach the computer. This is necessary only when the computer misrecognizes the same word repeatedly.

Commands should not be corrected or trained in the Correction window. To train commands, see page 175.

Teaching NaturallySpeaking a New Word

If you say a word NaturallySpeaking doesn't know, there's no special procedure to follow. Enter the word in the Correction window like you're fixing any other mistake, and the program will learn the new word automatically.

1. Say the new word. The computer will type it wrong.
2. Say "Correct That."
3. Type (or spell) the new word in the Correction window and press Enter.

So Many Options! Which Is Best?

Here are the easiest ways to correct mistakes:

If You Can Type

When You're Starting Out, Correct by Voice

Do your dictating in the NaturallySpeaking window to become familiar with its voice commands:

1. Say "Select" plus the words you want to correct.
2. Redictate what you actually said.

If NaturallySpeaking still types the wrong thing:

3. Say "Spell That a-b-c," spelling the first few letters of what you said. This opens the Correction window with these letters entered.
4. Press Alt+P to listen to your recorded voice.
5. Type what you actually said and press Enter.

Save and print your writing directly from the Naturally-Speaking window or copy and paste the text into another program. (Press Ctrl+A to Select All and Ctrl+C to Copy. Move to another program and press Ctrl+V to Paste.)

Later, Use the Keyboard and Mouse

After learning to correct by voice and teaching the computer to improve, switch to correcting by hand. Use NaturallySpeaking to dictate a draft into any Windows program, then edit the usual way—with keyboard and mouse. Use the Correction window occasionally, as needed, to teach NaturallySpeaking a new word or to correct a repeated misrecognition.

Review the Keyboard Editing Shortcuts table on page 52. Editing with the keyboard takes some practice but can be much more efficient than using the mouse.

Start correcting by keyboard after a few weeks of correcting by voice, or sooner if you are satisfied with your recognition accuracy. You can correct this way in any program.

If You Can't Type

If you can't type, do your dictating in the NaturallySpeaking window to become familiar with its voice commands.

1. Say "Select" plus the words you want to correct.
2. Redictate what you actually said.

If NaturallySpeaking still types the wrong thing:

3. Say "Spell That a-b-c," spelling the first few letters of what you said. This opens the Correction window with these letters entered.
4. Say "Click Play Back" to listen to your recorded voice.

5. Spell what you wanted typed, and edit if necessary. (If you can type at all, type here instead of spelling to avoid frustration.)
6. Say "Choose 1" to close the Correction window.

To move what you've dictated to another program, say:

1. "Copy All to Clipboard."
2. "Switch to Previous Window."
3. "Paste That."

Once you're familiar with correcting by voice, dictate and correct in Word, WordPerfect, or another Select-and-Say program if desired. See Chapter 6 for editing and formatting voice commands.

Active and Backup Vocabularies

As you speak, NaturallySpeaking compares what you say with more than 100,000 words in the computer's memory. This "active vocabulary" is stored in RAM for fast access.

When you spell or type a word in the Correction window, Naturally-Speaking lists ten alternatives that begin with the letters you've spelled. These alternatives are drawn from both the active vocabulary and a backup vocabulary, stored on disk. The huge backup vocabulary of over 230,000 words includes even arcane technical terms and proper names.

Usually you won't have to finish spelling a word in the Correction window before that word appears among the ten alternatives. If this occurs, the word you said was either in NaturallySpeaking's active or backup vocabulary. NaturallySpeaking might not have recognized it because the word wasn't "active." If the word you then choose in the Correction window is in the backup vocabulary, NaturallySpeaking will move it into the active vocabulary. This increases the chance that it will be recognized correctly next time.

There's a limit to how many words can be active at once. When a backup word is moved to active, the least-used active word is moved to the backup dictionary. NaturallySpeaking keeps track of which words are used most often, swapping words between active and backup transparently.

The Vocabulary Editor command in the NaturallySpeaking Tools menu shows many of the words in your active vocabulary. You can see words in the backup vocabulary only when they appear as alternatives in the Correction window, as you type the first few letters of the word.

To Correct or Not To Correct?

NaturallySpeaking's accuracy improves when you use the Correction window. However, you'll probably find it impractical to correct every last mistake this way. If you don't use the Correction window, the computer will not improve, but it also will not get worse.

Editing and Formatting

After you draft a letter or other document, you'll usually want to revise it. This chapter discusses editing—reorganizing and fine-tuning your words. It also covers using bold text, different fonts, and other formatting.

You can edit by voice, keyboard, mouse, or all three methods combined. When you're starting out, take the time to learn how to edit with voice commands. As you become more familiar with the software, make changes in the way that is most comfortable for you. See Chapter 12 for recommendations on what editing methods are best for different situations.

If you want to edit by voice, it's easiest to use a Select-and-Say application. If the application you want to use (such as an e-mail program) is not Select-and-Say, editing by keyboard and mouse will probably be easier. Alternately, you can edit your text by voice in the NaturallySpeaking window, then copy and paste it into the other application. See page 36 for a list of what applications are Select-and-Say.

When you're editing by voice, use any of the commands described in this chapter. However, do not use "Correct That." "Correct That," "Spell That" (its synonym), and the Correction window are reserved for instances when NaturallySpeaking misrecognizes what you said and types the wrong word. Chapter 5 discusses this kind of correction.

Select and Dictate

To revise and rewrite, simply select the text you want to fix—by voice, keyboard, or mouse—then dictate the new text. As with typing, the newly dictated text will replace the selection. Be sure, though, that NaturallySpeaking selects the correct block of text, so that other text is not inadvertently deleted.

If you've selected text and then dictate a word unintentionally, or if NaturallySpeaking misrecognizes a command, the selected text will disappear. Press Ctrl+Z to Undo (or choose Undo from the Edit menu).

Selecting by Voice

You can use two types of commands to select text by voice. The simplest commands select words verbatim—you say "Select" plus the words you want to change. You can use these commands only in Select-and-Say applications. These selection commands are described on page 37 and summarized below.

Example	*General form*
Select computer (where "computer" is the word you want to change)	Select \<text>
Select we to states (selects a range of words, from the first word to the second)	Select \<text> to \<text> Select \<text> through \<text>
Select Again (if the computer chooses the wrong occurrence of the word you said)	Select Again

The other selection commands use navigation language. First, move the cursor to the text you want to change by saying "Move," a direction, and how far to go. See the examples below. When you're next to the text to change, say "Select" plus the number of words, characters, or lines to be changed. Again, see the examples. These commands work in almost any Windows program.

Say this	Options
Moving	
Move Up 7 Lines	Move <Up/Down/Back/Forward>
Move Back 2 Paragraphs	<1-20> <Lines/Paragraphs>
Move Down a Line	Move <Up/Down/Back/Forward> a <Line/Paragraph>
Move Right 3 Characters	Move <Left/Right/Back/Forward> <1-20> <Words/Characters>
Move Back a Word	Move <Left/Right/Back/Forward> a <Word/Character/Line/Paragraph>
Go to Top of Document	<Go/Move> to
Move to Beginning of Line	<Top/Bottom/Start/Beginning/End> of <Document/Line/Paragraph>
Go to Top	Go to <Top/Bottom> (goes to top or bottom of document)
Selecting	
Select Last 3 Words	Select <Next/Last/Previous/
Select Back 2 Paragraphs	Forward/Back> <1-20> <Words/Paragraphs/Characters>
Select Word	Select <Word/Paragraph>
Select Next Paragraph	Select <Next/Last/Previous/ Forward/Back> <Word/Paragraph>
Select Document	
Select All	
Select That	selects the last phrase you said

When you've selected the words you want to change, dictate (or type) the revised text. The new text will replace the selection.

Selecting by Mouse

Using the mouse is the easiest way to select—just drag the mouse across the text you want to change. Selecting by mouse is often slower, however, than using the keyboard.

There are a few mouse shortcuts. In many programs you can select one word by double-clicking on that word. In some programs, such as Microsoft Word and WordPerfect, you can select a whole line by clicking in the left margin next to that line.

Keyboard Editing Shortcuts

If you prefer to edit by typing, speed your work by using keyboard shortcuts. These shortcuts work in almost any Windows program, and they will dramatically slash the time and keystrokes you spend editing. Take the time to learn them—ten minutes spent practicing with these keys can save you many hours in editing.

Press these keys	To do this
Ctrl	**hold down the Ctrl key to move by jumps, instead of one character at a time**
Ctrl+Left (Left Arrow key) Ctrl+Right (Right Arrow key)	move cursor by one word at a time
Ctrl+Up (Up Arrow key) Ctrl+Down (Down Arrow key)	move cursor by one paragraph at a time
Ctrl+Backspace	delete word to the left of cursor
Ctrl+Delete	delete word to the right of cursor
Shift	**hold down the Shift key to select as you move**
Shift+Left, Shift+Right	select one character at a time
Shift+Up, Shift+Down	select one line at a time
Ctrl+Shift	**hold down the Ctrl and Shift keys together to select in jumps**
Ctrl+Shift+Left Ctrl+Shift+Right	select one word at a time
Ctrl+Shift+Up Ctrl+Shift+Down	select one paragraph at a time
Backspace key	delete left
Delete key	delete right
Home key	skip to start of line
End key	skip to end of line
Shift+Home	select to start of line
Shift+End	select to end of line
Also available	
Ctrl+Home	skip to start of document
Ctrl+End	skip to end of document

| Ctrl+Shift+Home | select to start of document |
| Ctrl+Shift+End | select to end of document |

More Editing Commands

Selecting and dictating is not the only way to revise. You can delete, copy, cut, paste, and move the cursor to right where you want it.

Example commands	*Variations, or what the command does*
Deleting	
Scratch That	deletes the last word or phrase you dictated, or what's selected
Delete That	deletes the last word or phrase you dictated, or what's selected
Delete Last 3 Words Delete Back 2 Paragraphs	Delete <Last/Next/Previous /Forward/Back> <1-20> <Words/Paragraphs/Characters>
Delete Word	Delete <Word/Paragraph>
Delete Next Paragraph	Delete <Last/Next/Previous /Forward/Back> <Word/Paragraph/Character>
Backspace	Deletes previous character
Backspace 5	Backspace <2-20>
Undo	**reverses the last action**
Undo That Undo Last Action	note: It's more reliable to undo mistakes by hand than by voice; choose Undo from the Edit menu (in most programs), or press Ctrl+Z
Cut and Paste	
Copy That	copies the selected text to the clipboard
Cut That	moves the selected text to the clipboard
Paste That	pastes the clipboard text into the document
Moving the Cursor	
Insert Before New York	Insert Before <text> (puts the cursor just before <text>)
Insert After Albuquerque	Insert After <text> (puts the cursor just after <text>)

Insert Before That	puts the cursor at the start of the selection
Insert After That	puts the cursor at the end of the selection

Practice these commands in the NaturallySpeaking window to learn how they work. Sometimes they work differently, or don't work at all, in other programs. By learning in the Naturally-Speaking window, you'll know what is supposed to happen when you say each command.

"Resume With" Command

Use the "Resume With" command when you change your mind or misspeak while you're dictating. It's best suited for editing as you're composing rather than editing already completed text.

To use this command, say "Resume With" plus a word or two you just spoke, then the new text you want to say. Here's a example of how the process works.

Do this	The computer shows
Say "I enjoyed talking on the phone with you today"	I enjoyed talking on the phone with you today
You change your mind—you want it to say "visiting" instead of "talking on the phone"	
Say "Resume With enjoyed visiting with you today" (say this without pausing)	I enjoyed visiting with you today

Here's how NaturallySpeaking interprets "Resume With enjoyed visiting with you today." The key words "Resume With" tell NaturallySpeaking that you're not just dictating, you're saying this particular command. NaturallySpeaking searches backwards in your document to find whatever the next word is—in this case "enjoyed." It deletes all text beyond "enjoyed." NaturallySpeaking then types the rest of what you said, "visiting with you today."

What Is "That"?

The word "That" in voice commands refers to the text selected. If no text is selected, "That" refers to the last phrase you dictated.

Phrases are separated by your pauses. If you dictate a whole paragraph without pausing, then pause and say "Scratch That," NaturallySpeaking will erase the whole paragraph. If you pause after each word, then pause and say "Scratch That," Naturally-Speaking will erase only the last word you said.

Formatting

The NaturallySpeaking word processor works well for simple tasks, such as letters and memos. Lack of page numbering and double-spacing are its most immediate limitations. In the NaturallySpeaking window, use these commands to change formatting.

Bold, Italics, and Underline

Select some text, then say:

- ▶ "Bold That"
- ▶ "Italicize That"
- ▶ "Underline That"
- ▶ "Restore That" (to return to plain text)

Fonts

To change fonts, say "Set Font" or "Format That" plus the name of a font, a size, or a style, as shown:

Say one of these	Plus one of these typefaces	Plus a size	Plus a style
Set Font	Arial	4 to 120	Bold
Format That	Courier		Italics
	Times		Underline
	Times New		Plain
	Roman		Plain Text
			Regular

You can specify just a typeface, just a style, or a combination. Use "Format That" instead of "Set Font" in any of these commands if you prefer.

Example	General form
Set Font Times	Set Font <typeface>
Set Font Times 12	Set Font <typeface> <size>
Set Font Times 12 Bold	Set Font <typeface> <size> <style>
Set Font Times Bold	Set Font <typeface> <style>
Set Font Bold	Set Font <style>

To change just the size of a font, use the commands "Set Size" or "Format That Size."

Example	General form
Set Size 18	Set Size <4 *to* 120>
Format That Size 12	Format That Size <4 *to* 120>

Uppercase, Lowercase, and Titles

Say one of these	To do this
Cap That Format That Cap Format That Caps Format That Capitals Format That Initial Caps	capitalize the first letter of each word, except small words ("the," "of," etc.); this is especially useful for dictating titles
All Caps That Format That All Caps Format That Uppercase	change to all uppercase
No Caps That Format That No Caps Format That Lowercase	change to all lowercase

The easiest way to dictate a title:

1. Pause briefly.
2. Say the title.
3. Pause.
4. Say "Cap That."

See Chapter 8 for commands that let you capitalize as you dictate, instead of after the fact.

Left, Right, Center, and Bullets

Say one of these	To do this
Left Align That Format That Left Aligned	make paragraph flush left
Right Align That Format That Right Aligned	make paragraph flush right
Center That Format That Centered	make paragraph centered
Format That Bullet Style	make paragraph bulleted; to remove bullets, repeat command

Hyphenation and Removing Spaces

Say one of these	To do this
Compound That Format That Without Spaces	take out the spaces between words
Hyphenate That Format That With Hyphens	add hyphens between words (not within words)

Spelling Out Numbers

If you say "seventeen," NaturallySpeaking takes its best guess at whether you want to type "17" or "seventeen." You can change from the digits to words and back with the commands "Format That Number" and "Format That Spelled Out." Simply select the text to change, then say either of these two commands.

Say this	To do this
Format That Number	Change words to digits
Format That Spelled Out	Change digits to words

When Is Each Command Available?

Many commands are available in some programs but not others. This table summarizes when each correction and editing option is available.

Ways of correcting	Available in the NaturallySpeaking window and other Select-and-Say programs	Available in other Windows programs
Keyboard and mouse	yes	yes
Select and delete by character, word, and paragraph	yes	yes
Select words by saying "Select" plus the words you want	yes	no
Use "Insert Before/After," "Resume With"	yes	no
Use "Bold That" and other formatting commands	some programs— try it and see	no
Use the Correction window to teach the computer ("Correct That")	yes	yes, but only for the most recent phrase you've said
Other commands	yes	sometimes—try it

Recommendations for Commands

▶ If a command doesn't work, try a different version of it. NaturallySpeaking recognizes long words better than short words. If "Select Back 3 Words" doesn't work, try "Select Previous 3 Words."

▶ Avoid the Delete commands, except "Delete That." Delete in two steps. First, select what you want to erase. Then say "Delete That." This prevents the computer from acting out "Delete Next 22 Paragraphs" when you actually said "Delete Next 2 Paragraphs."

▶ If you want to undo, don't do it by voice. Press Ctrl+Z instead, or choose Undo from the Edit menu. It's too easy for NaturallySpeaking to misunderstand you and prevent you from going back.

NaturallySpeaking in Different Programs

In the NaturallySpeaking window, in Word and WordPerfect, and in other Select-and-Say applications, NaturallySpeaking has full information about what words are on the screen. If you say "Select Boston," NaturallySpeaking knows just where to go. If you select some words by keyboard or mouse, then say "Correct That," NaturallySpeaking knows what words are selected.

In other programs, however, such as Eudora and Excel, NaturallySpeaking can't tell what words are on the screen, except for the most recent phrase you've said. You can say "Correct That," but it will only correct the last thing you said.

To see if a particular command is available in the application you're using, say the command while holding down the Ctrl key. This will force NaturallySpeaking to recognize your speech as a command. If nothing happens after you say the command with the Ctrl key held down, the command you said is not available in that application. If you test commands without holding down the Ctrl key, NaturallySpeaking may type text instead of executing a command. In this case, you won't know whether the command's failure was because the command is not available or because NaturallySpeaking misrecognized what you said.

7

Web Surfing, Word, and WordPerfect

While NaturallySpeaking is running, you can dictate text, open menus, and give computer commands by voice, in virtually any Windows program. In several special programs, however, you have even more control and flexibility. In Microsoft Internet Explorer, you can browse the World Wide Web by voice. Just say the name of a link to click on it. In Microsoft Word and Corel WordPerfect, you can select text by voice, use the Correction window easily, and use more voice commands than you can in other applications. In this chapter, you'll learn how to work with these three special voice-enabled programs.

Surfing the Web

With any Web browser, you can use NaturallySpeaking to fill out forms, open menus, and click links using MouseGrid (described on page 93). It's much easier, though, to use NaturallySpeaking's built-in Web commands, which let you click on a link by just saying its name. To use this special "surf-by-voice" capacity, you must use Microsoft Internet Explorer as your browser. "Surf-by-voice" works with Internet Explorer versions 4.0 and later. Internet Explorer can be downloaded free from the Microsoft Web site, www.microsoft.com.

NaturalWeb

NaturallySpeaking communicates with Internet Explorer through a software link called "NaturalWeb." If you have Internet Explorer installed already, this link installed automatically when you originally installed NaturallySpeaking. If you installed Internet Explorer after NaturallySpeaking, re-run the Naturally-Speaking installation program, adding only the "NaturalWeb" part of the program. (To do this, insert the NaturallySpeaking CD-ROM and follow the on-screen instructions.) You can tell if NaturalWeb is installed by looking for it in the Start Menu under Programs, Dragon NaturallySpeaking. If there's an item listed called "NaturalWeb," it is installed.

Quick Reference: Surfing by Voice

To use the Web by voice, start NaturallySpeaking first. After NaturallySpeaking has finished loading, start Internet Explorer.

Here is a summary of the most useful commands for Web surfing, followed by a detailed discusson of each.

To do this	Say this
Click on a link	The name of the link, or a portion of the name
Go to a "Favorite" page	Go to name of Favorite
Go back a page	Go Back
Go forward a page	Go Forward
Go to your home page	Go Home
Stop a page from loading	Stop Loading
Scroll up one screen	Page Up

Scroll down one screen	Page Down
Enter a Web address (URL)	Go to address (pause), *Say the address* (pause), Go There
Select images	Image *or* Click Image
Select check boxes	Check Box *or* Click Check Box
Select radio buttons	Radio Button *or* Check Radio Button
Move between links, images, check boxes, or radio buttons	Next *or* Previous
Choose a link, image, check box, or radio button	Click That One *or* Click That *or* That One
Dictate into a text box or form	Type Text *or* Edit Box *or* Text Field

Links and Buttons

To click a link by voice, just say the name of it. You don't need to say the whole name—just enough so that NaturallySpeaking can tell it apart from the other link names.

When NaturallySpeaking hears the link name, a small arrow flashes to show what link the computer heard (Figure 7-1). If NaturallySpeaking chooses the wrong link, say "Go Back" to return to the previous Web page. Then say the link name again. You can say "Click" before the link name if you want, and sometimes this helps NaturallySpeaking recognize the link name better.

Figure 7-1
An arrow flashes to confirm what link the computer heard.

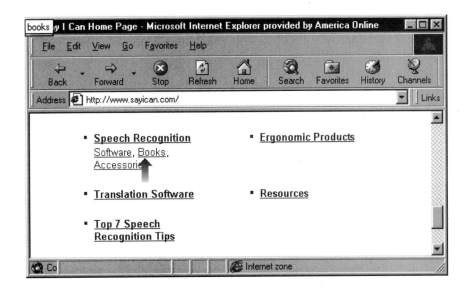

Figure 7-2
A question
mark appears
meaning, "Is
this the link
you want?"
Say "Click
That One" if it
is, "Next" if
not.

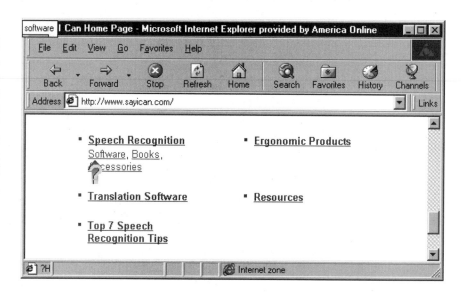

Sometimes NaturallySpeaking isn't sure what link you meant. It will show a question mark, as in Figure 7-2. Say "Next" or "Previous" to move the question mark to the next or previous links, if necessary. Then say "Click That One" to active the link the question mark is next to. You can also say "Click That" or "That One."

Buttons work similarly to links. To click on a button, say the button name. In Figure 7-3, you could say "Place Order" to press the Place Order button.

Figure 7-3
To press a
standard button,
say the button's
name.

Only buttons that look like the buttons in Figure 7-3 can be activated by saying the button name. Many buttons on Web pages are drawn by the Web site's artist or designer, such as the ones shown in Figure 7-4. These buttons cannot be read by NaturallySpeaking. To press them, use the MouseGrid commands.

Figure 7-4
Graphical
buttons like
these can't be
activated by
saying the button
name.

Images

To make NaturallySpeaking pay attention to the images on a page, say "Image" or "Click Image." An arrow points to the first

image on the page. Say "Next" and "Previous" to move the arrow among different images, then say "That One" to click on the image the arrow points to.

Favorites

Favorites, also called bookmarks, are sites you tell your browser to keep track of so you can locate them easily. In Internet Explorer, you can click on the "Favorites" button to see the sites in this list. NaturallySpeaking lets you jump to any of these sites easily. Say "Go to Favorite" plus the site name, exactly as it appears in the Favorites menu. For example, you could say "Go to Favorite Yahoo" if Yahoo were one of the items in your Favorites list.

To add to the Favorites list by voice, be sure you are looking at the Web page you want to add. Then say "Click Favorites" to open the Favorites menu in Internet Explorer. Say "Add to Favorites," and the Add Favorites dialog box will open. Type a name for this page (you can't dictate here). Save the page and click the OK button, or say "Click OK."

Entering a Web Address

You can enter a Web address, or URL, into Internet Explorer by saying "Go to Address." Then dictate the web address, as you would normally speak it. For example, for the Say I Can Web site, say "w w w dot say I can dot com." Uppercase and lowercase don't matter—both work the same. After entering the URL, say "Go There" or "Click Go," which acts like pressing the Enter key. For more examples of how to dictate Web addresses, see page 80.

Browser Commands

You can push the browser control buttons by voice with the commands listed here.

To click this button	Say this
Back	Go Back
Forward	Go Forward
Stop	Stop Loading
Refresh	Refresh
Home	Go Home

Check Boxes and Radio Buttons

To make NaturallySpeaking pay attention to check boxes, say "Check Box" or "Click Check Box." An arrow appears by the first check box. Say "Next" or "Previous" to move the arrow to the box you want, then say "That One" or "Click That."

Radio buttons work the same way. Say "Radio Button" to make NaturallySpeaking point at a radio button. Say "Next" or "Previous" as many times as necessary, then say "That One" or "Click That."

Text Boxes

You can dictate into any text field on a Web page, such as a form requesting your name and address. To move to the first text box on a page, say "Type Text" or "Edit Box" or "Text Field." Say "Next" or "Previous" to move through fields. You can dictate text whenever your flashing cursor is in a text box—the computer acts as if you're typing. Dictating in text boxes, you can correct and edit by voice, as described in Chapters 5 and 6.

Scrolling

To move up or down one screen of information, say "Page Up" or "Page Down." To move line by line, say "Line Up" or "Line Down." Say "Go to Top" or "Go to Bottom" to move to the top or bottom of the page.

You can make the page move, or scroll, automatically by saying "Start Scrolling Up" or "Start Scrolling Down." Say "Speed Up" or "Slow Down" to change the scrolling speed. To stop, say "Stop Scrolling." You can even say the names of links while they are scrolling by.

Tips on Browsing the Web by Voice

▶ For maximum efficiency, create shortcuts for your name, address, phone number, e-mail address, and other information you frequently enter on Web forms. No more tedious typing! (For detailed instructions on how to create shortcuts, see Chapter 10, "Automate Your Work.")

▶ Some browse-by-voice features, like saying the names of links, are easy. Others, like saying "Next" and "Previous" repeatedly, become tedious if you're able to use a mouse. Feel free to mix voice, mouse, and keyboard, using just the commands you find most useful.

▶ Drop-down lists cannot be activated by voice.

▶ If you have a hand injury that makes clicking the mouse painful, consider moving the mouse by hand, but clicking by voice, especially to click on images and checkboxes. See page 93 for instructions on how to click the mouse by voice.

Word and WordPerfect

To use voice commands in Microsoft Word and Corel WordPerfect, you'll need NaturalWord, a software link that connects to your word processor and gives NaturallySpeaking information about what's on the screen. This link installed automatically when you originally installed NaturallySpeaking. To use the NaturalWord link and the additional voice commands it provides, you must have Word 97, Word 2000, WordPerfect 8, or WordPerfect 9.

If NaturalWord is installed properly, a new menu, "Dragon NaturallySpeaking," will appear in your word processor. You can use this same menu to access all NaturallySpeaking commands. (If the Dragon NaturallySpeaking menu is not in the menu bar of your word processor, see the troubleshooting suggestions on page 254.)

Turn the microphone on and off with the numeric "+" key, or click the small microphone icon next to the on-screen clock. As you dictate, the NaturallySpeaking Results box appears in the upper-left corner of the word processor window and the words you say are typed into your document.

For Best Performance

Many users find that their systems are more stable when they follow these steps in order:

1. Start NaturallySpeaking.
2. Start Word or WordPerfect.
3. Activate NaturalWord.

For best performance:

- ▸ Run only NaturallySpeaking and your word processor, with no other programs open.
- ▸ Disable your word processor's "check as you go" automatic grammar and spell checking.
- ▸ If you're using Word, turn off AutoCorrect. (From the Tools menu, choose AutoCorrect and turn off all the check boxes on the AutoCorrect tab.)
- ▸ Divide large documents into smaller documents of 50 pages or less.
- ▸ Have more than 64 MB of RAM.

Natural Language Commands

Beyond NaturallySpeaking's own commands, Word includes many additional commands for easy editing and formatting. These extra commands are called "natural language commands" on the assumption that you can give the computer commands "naturally," without having to remember what specific command to say. (These extra commands are not available in WordPerfect.)

To make NaturallySpeaking do what you want, however, you can't say just anything. Consider what you would instinctively say to have the computer make a table. Would it be one of these phrases?

- ▸ "insert a table"
- ▸ "create a table"
- ▸ "make a new table"
- ▸ "start a table"

If you would say one of these phrases, NaturallySpeaking will do what you want. But if your natural command is "put a new table here," the program won't recognize it.

It's not necessary or useful to learn every voice command variation available. Find a way of saying commands that's easy to remember and that works for NaturallySpeaking. To make a table, for example, say whatever phrase comes to mind. If it doesn't work, press Ctrl+Z to undo and say the command another way. When you find a variation that works, keep using it. Here are some commands that do work, to give you ideas.

Copying, Moving, Cutting, Pasting, and Deleting

Select Next 10 Paragraphs

Cut Them

Copy This Page

Delete Next Paragraph

Move Next 5 Lines to Top of Document

Move Next 4 Sentences Down 3 Paragraphs

Move Up 5 Pages

Go to Last Page

Go to Top of Document

Delete the Previous 2 Sentences

There are many variations on these commands as well.

▶ Possible actions include select, cut, copy, move, delete, and paste.
▶ Items to act on include characters, words, lines, sentences, paragraphs, pages, and cells (table cells).
▶ Numbers in these commands can be 1 to 20.

Spelling, Grammar, and Printing

Check Spelling

Run Spell Check

Check Grammar

Print Preview

Print Pages 1 Through 5 (can use numbers up to 100)

Print This Page

Print Document

Tables

Insert a 2 by 7 Table

Add a Table With 4 Rows and 3 Columns

Cut This Column

Insert a Row

Insert 4 Rows

Formatting

Make This Paragraph Times Italics

Format That Bold *or* Bold That

Format That 12 Point
Make Last Sentence Uppercase
Make This Line Capitalized *or* Capitalize This Line
Make This Paragraph Red
Set This Paragraph Double Spaced
Add Border
Start a Page
Start a Section
Insert Numbers
Make This Paragraph Two Columns
Double-Space the Last Three Paragraphs
Turn the Next 5 Lines Into a Bulleted List

All the commands discussed in Chapter 6, "Editing and Formatting," work in Word and WordPerfect, too. For more examples of natural language commands, review the Naturally-Speaking online Help—look under the headings Natural Language Commands and What Can I Say.

Making Natural Language Commands Practical

Sometimes you'll tell the computer what you want to do and it will work perfectly. These moments capture the thrill and drama of voice-activated computing. To make natural language commands work smoothly:

▶ When a command does the wrong thing, immediately use your word processor's Undo command.
▶ Stay away from commands that select and act in the same command. (For example, "Delete Next 7 Paragraphs.") The computer might select the wrong text, then act on it anyway—it might delete 17 paragraphs. Instead, use two commands—one to select and the other to act. Say "Select Next 7 Paragraphs." Check that the computer did it correctly, then say "Delete That."

Troubleshooting

Using natural language commands can be frustrating. Often you'll say a command that doesn't work as you expect. Watch the Results box to see if NaturallySpeaking recognized your command accurately. This helps determine whether you said a command that does not exist, whether NaturallySpeaking misrecognized your words, or whether NaturallySpeaking recognized your words correctly but executed incorrectly.

- ▶ If the Results box shows words other than what you said, use Train Words (page 175) to teach NaturallySpeaking how you say the command, then try again.
- ▶ If the Results box shows the command you said with each word capitalized, NaturallySpeaking heard and executed the command. Or it tried to execute it but couldn't because of what you were doing in the word processor at the time. For example, saying "Insert a Table" will not work if you're already inside a table.
- ▶ If the Results box has the command you said with the words in lowercase, NaturallySpeaking recognized the words right, but the command you said is not available or does not exist.

Hold down the Ctrl key as you speak to force NaturallySpeaking to recognize what you say as a command. If you say a command with the Ctrl key held down and nothing happens, that command is probably not available.

8

Numbers, Punctuation, and Capitalization

This chapter describes how to dictate numbers, punctuation, capitalization, Web addresses, and a few other special items.

Numbers

Numbers

To dictate a number, just say it. NaturallySpeaking will type either the digit ("5") or the word ("five"), making a guess of which you intended. To force NaturallySpeaking to type a digit instead of a word (for numbers 0 to 9), say "numeral" plus the number ("numeral 2"). This tip is especially useful when dictating the digits 2 and 4, which are usually mistaken for "to" and "for" unless you say "numeral 2" and "numeral 4."

NaturallySpeaking adds commas to numbers of five digits or more (such as 21,469), but not four digit numbers (2146). To add a comma to a four digit number, say "comma" where you want the comma. See the table below for examples. For a decimal point, just say "point." If you dictate a Zip code, Naturally-Speaking knows not to add a comma and formats the Zip code correctly.

To type	Say any of these
315	three hundred fifteen three one five three fifteen
809	eight-hundred nine eight zero nine eight oh nine
1485	one thousand four hundred eighty-five fourteen eighty-five
1,485	one comma four hundred eighty five one comma four eight five one comma four eighty-five
809,212	eight hundred and nine thousand two hundred twelve eight zero nine comma two one two
51.2	fifty-one point two five one point two
.2	point two
0.102	zero point one oh two
500	five hundred
5000	five thousand
90,210	ninety thousand two hundred ten
90210 *(Zip code)*	nine oh two one oh
90210-1164 *(Zip code)*	nine oh two one oh hyphen one one six four
75%	seventy-five percent sign
$99	ninety-nine dollars
$99.10	ninety-nine dollars and ten cents
$8.2 million	eight point two million dollars

After dictating a number, you can change it from digits to words by saying "Format That Spelled Out." You can change from words to digits by saying "Format That Number." These commands also change ordinal words, like "first" and "tenth" to "1st" and "10th." They change currency too: "80 cents" becomes "$.80" and "200 dollars" becomes "$200."

Dates

Dictate dates as you would usually speak them:

To type	Say this
April 21, 2000	April twenty-one comma two thousand (*not* April twenty-first)
7/6/96	seven slash six slash ninety-six

Times

Say times as you would usually speak them.

To type	Say this
5:00	five o'clock
5:00 AM	five o'clock a m
3:17 PM	three seventeen p m

If what you dictate includes "a.m." "p.m." or "o'clock," NaturallySpeaking adds a colon automatically. Otherwise you must say the colon ("three colon thirty" for 3:30). If you didn't say the colon, NaturallySpeaking wouldn't know you wanted a time and would type the number 330.

You can change the labels AM and PM to something else if you like (for example, "a.m." and "p.m."). To do this, from the Start Menu choose Settings, Control Panel, Regional Settings, then click the Time tab and change the AM and PM symbols as you prefer.

Phone Numbers

To dictate phone numbers, just say the phone number. It will usually be formatted correctly, with dashes separating the number groups.

To type	Say this
510-555-1212	five one oh five five five one two one two

If you want different punctuation, say:

▶ "hyphen" for "-"
▶ "open paren" and "close paren" for "(" and ")"

To type	Say this
555-1212	five five five hyphen one two one two five fifty-five hyphen twelve twelve
(510) 555-1212	open paren five one oh close paren five five five hyphen one two one two

Fractions

To dictate the most common fractions, just say them as you normally would. This applies if the denominator (bottom) is 1 through 10, or 16.

To type	Say this
1/2	one half
5/7	five sevenths
15/16	fifteen sixteenths
3 3/8	three and three eighths

For all fractions, say "slash" or "over" where you want the slash in the fraction. The numerator (top) can be up to 199, and the denominator (bottom) has no size limit.

To type	Say this
5/12	five over twelve
6 10/99	six space bar ten slash ninety-nine
3/8	three slash eight
110/180	one ten over one eighty

Roman Numerals

These commands type Roman numerals:

To type	Say this
I	roman one
II	roman two
III	roman three
IV	roman four
V	roman five
VI	roman six
VII	roman seven
VIII	roman eight
IX	roman nine
X	roman ten
XX to XC	roman twenty to roman ninety *by tens*
C	roman one hundred
CC to CM	roman two hundred *to* roman nine hundred *by hundreds*
M	roman one thousand
MM	roman two thousand
MMM	roman three thousand

String together the commands above to get the number you want:

XXXVIII (38)	roman thirty roman eight
MCMLXIX (1969)	roman one thousand roman nine hundred roman sixty roman nine

Punctuation

To type	Say this
Most common	
,	comma
.	period
	dot
	point
	(each one has different spacing characteristics)
?	question mark

!	exclamation mark
	exclamation point
"	open quote
	close quote
`	open single quote
	close single quote
(	open paren
	open parenthesis
	left paren
)	close paren
	close parenthesis
	right paren
'	apostrophe
's	apostrophe-ess
-	hyphen
	minus sign
-- (double hyphen)	dash
	space bar

Less common

&	ampersand
	and sign
*	asterisk
@	at sign
`	backquote
\	backslash
^	caret
[	open bracket
	left bracket
]	close bracket
	right bracket
{	open brace
	left brace
}	close brace
	right brace
<	less than
	open angle bracket
>	greater than
	close angle bracket
:	colon
;	semicolon
$	dollar sign
...	ellipsis

=	equal sign
#	number sign
	pound sign
%	percent sign
~	tilde
_	underscore
|	vertical bar
:-)	smiley face

Possessives

Say "apostrophe" or "apostrophe-ess" as needed. Say it right after the word, without pausing.

To type	Say this
boat's	boat apostrophe-ess
girls'	girls apostrophe

Adding Spaces and Removing Spaces

- "Space Bar" acts like pressing the space bar.
- "No Space" before a word omits the space between words. This is especially useful for typing a compound word, such as "bullfeathers" (say "bull No Space feathers"). (You could also say "bullfeathers" normally and add it as a new word in the Correction window if you'll be saying it more than once.)
- "No Space On" disables automatic spacing: thisiswhatyouget. "No Space Off" returns formatting to normal.
- "Compound That" removes spaces from the last thing you said.

To type	Say this
OpenAccess	Cap open Cap access (pause) Compound That

It's easier, though, to say "no space" while dictating.

OpenAccess	Cap open no space Cap access

NaturallySpeaking types two spaces after the end of a sentence. You can change this to one space using the Options command in the NaturallySpeaking Tools menu (see page 218).

Hyphenated Words

Say common hyphenated words normally. For example, "door-to-door," "time-share."

To type a hyphen, say "hyphen."

To type	Say this
first-time skier	first hyphen time skier

E-mail and Web Addresses

Dictate e-mail and Web addresses by saying them as you normally would.

To type	Say this
socks@whitehouse.gov	socks at-sign white house dot gov
http://www.SayIcan.com	h t t p w w w dot say I can dot com

NaturallySpeaking automatically recognizes these words as part of Internet addresses: "com," "org," "gov," "net," "mil," and "sys." Also, these words if you spell them out: "e d u," "c a," "c o," and "u k." The program knows you're dictating a Web address if what you say starts with "h t t p," "w w w," or "web." To change capitalization of e-mail and Web addresses, use the capitalization voice commands described later in this chapter.

For any e-mail or Web address you'll be using three times or more, create a dictation shorthand for it. That way you can say "Christopher's e-mail address" to get the text you want—you avoid having to dictate the whole address and punctuation each time. For detailed instructions on creating shorthands, see Chapter 10.

Special Characters

There's a special procedure to dictate certain unusual characters (such as these: ©¶§÷½¥) and accented and international characters (such as these: úÑæî). For each character you want to use in regular dictation, you need to do a one-time process of adding that character to your personal vocabulary. In your document, or the NaturallySpeaking window, follow these steps:

1. Say the character name (such as "paragraph sign"). See page 42 for a list of character names, or search for "spelling characters" in NaturallySpeaking's online help.
2. The computer will type the name, not the character. Say "Correct That" to open the Correction Window.
3. Say the character name again. This will enter the character in the Correction window. If you get the wrong character, press the Backspace key to delete it and try again.
4. Say "Choose 1" or press Enter. The Correction window closes, the special character appears in your document, and you've added this character to your dictation vocabulary. Be sure to save your speech files to make this change permanent.

Capitalization

You can change capitalization while dictating. Some commands work for just the next word you dictate, while others remain in effect until canceled. You can also change the capitalization of text that's already dictated.

NaturallySpeaking will automatically capitalize proper names and the first word in a sentence. Some words have both uppercase and lowercase forms, and NaturallySpeaking will take a guess based on context. If the program types the wrong capitalization, correct it manually or teach the computer in the Correction window.

To Modify the Next Word

▶ "Cap" will make the next word appear with its first letter capitalized. It's as if you held the Shift key down for the word's first letter.
▶ "All Caps" will type the next word you say all UPPERCASE.
▶ "No Caps" will force the next word to be lowercase.

To type	Say this
Her last name was Lake.	her last name was Cap lake period
naturallyspeaking	No Caps NaturallySpeaking

To type the word "cap" instead of the command (as in "baseball cap"), pause after saying it. To type a word with a capital letter in the middle of it, like "WordPerfect," teach "WordPerfect" to the computer as a new word by saying it once then using the Correction window.

To Modify Several Words

▶ "Caps On" will Capitalize the First Letter of Each Word. This is especially useful for dictating titles. Naturally-Speaking knows not to capitalize prepositions and articles, such as "in" and "the." "Caps Off" returns capitalization to normal.

▶ "All Caps On" will type ALL UPPERCASE. "All Caps Off" returns capitalization to normal.

▶ "No Caps On" will type all lowercase words. "No Caps Off" returns capitalization to normal.

To type	Say this
The Catcher in the Rye	Caps On the catcher in the rye Caps Off

Capitalization automatically returns to normal if you move in your document.

You can use commands that modify a single word ("No Caps") even while a command that modifies several word ("Caps On") is active.

To type:	Say this:
The CATCHER in the Rye	Caps On the All Caps catcher in the rye Caps Off

To Modify Text After It's Been Typed

Say "Cap That," "All Caps That," or "No Caps That" to change what's already on the screen. If text is selected, the selected text will be changed. If no words are selected, the last phrase you dictated will be changed. Like other formatting commands:

▶ Pause before and after saying these commands.
▶ They will modify the last phrase you said, in any program.
▶ They will modify selected text only in Select-and-Say programs, including the NaturallySpeaking window.

For more details on formatting commands, see Chapter 6.

These three commands are quite useful—especially "Cap That." Even if you forget to say a capitalization command as you're dictating, you can easily correct afterwards without redictating what you said.

To type	Say this
The Catcher in the Rye	the catcher in the rye (pause) Cap That

Hands-Free Computing

Speech recognition is useful not only for dictation and formatting. You can control almost everything on your computer with NaturallySpeaking voice commands. This chapter tells you how.

If you have hand difficulties that limit typing, learn and practice with the commands in this chapter. If you are able to type, using voice commands is a matter of personal preference. Some people prefer to select menu commands and buttons with the keyboard and mouse. Others enjoy the convenience of ordering the computer to "Close Window" or "Click OK."

The Most Useful Voice Commands

The voice commands detailed in this section work in most programs, but practice them in the NaturallySpeaking window first until you're comfortable with them.

If you have Windows 95 or 98 and the program you're running uses "standard" menus and dialog boxes, Naturally-Speaking will let you activate the menus and controls by voice, even if NaturallySpeaking has never seen the program before. Commands that track menu names and dialog boxes do not work in Windows NT, however. For technical details, see "When Do Commands Work?" below.

When Do Commands Work?

When you start a program—even one you've never used before—NaturallySpeaking keeps track of the menu names in the program automatically. When you say "click" plus the name of a menu, Naturally-Speaking compares what you said to the menus names in the program. If what you said matches a menu name, NaturallySpeaking opens that menu.

Dialog boxes work the same way. When a dialog box opens, NaturallySpeaking recognizes the names of all the controls. It activates the appropriate control when you say the name.

NaturallySpeaking cannot recognize menus and controls from their graphic representation on the screen. The software needs this information in a program-readable form. For this, NaturallySpeaking relies on a part of the Windows operating system called Active Accessibility. This feature of Microsoft Windows maintains a view of what's on the screen in a form that computer programs can easily recognize.

Commands that track menu names and dialog boxes do not work in Windows NT because that operating system does not include the Active Accessibility feature. Also, programs that use nonstandard menus and controls do not provide information to Active Accessibility, so Naturally-Speaking will not recognize the menu and control names when you say them.

If you can't activate a menu or dialog box by saying "click" plus its name, review the section "Activating Commands by Saying Key Names," below.

Choosing Menu Commands

Say "click" plus the name of a menu to open it. Once the menu is open, say "click" plus the command name as it appears on the menu.

Say this	To do this
Click Edit (pause) Click Select All	choose the Select All command

In some programs you can leave out the second "click" and get the same result.

Click Edit (pause) Select All	Choose the Select All command

Say "Click Cancel" when a menu is open and you want to close it without choosing a command.

A few menu commands contain punctuation. Say the punctuation aloud.

Say this	For this command (once the menu is open)
Click Flip slash Rotate	Flip/Rotate

This example is from the program Paint, included with Windows.

Pressing Buttons

Say "Click" plus the name of the button.

▶ Examples: "Click OK," "Click Cancel," "Click Save," "Click Yes."

Other Controls

In dialog boxes, say "Click" plus the name of the control. See Figure 9-1 for a sample dialog box and what you can say. To check or uncheck the Collate checkbox, for example, say "Click Collate."

Figure 9-1
Some available
voice commands
include
"Click Properties,"
"Click All,"
"Click Pages,"
"Click Number of
Copies,"
"Click Cancel," and
"Click OK."

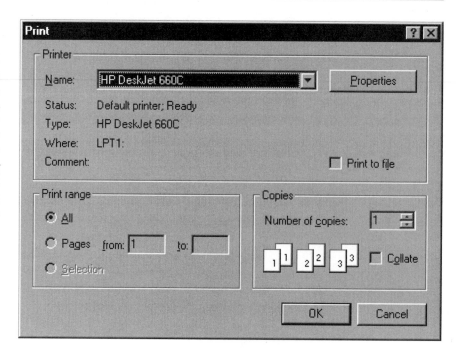

File and folder names and items in lists can't be said by voice.

Controlling Windows and Applications

Say any of these	To do this
Click Minimize Click System Menu (pause) Minimize	minimize the active widow
Click Maximize	maximize the active window
Click Restore	restore window to previous size
Click Close Press Alt F4	close the active program
Press Control F4	close the active document, not the whole program (works in many programs)
Click Start Menu Click Start Press Control Escape	open the Windows Start Menu

To switch between programs:

Switch to Next Window	switch to the next program
Switch to Previous Window	switch to the previous program

Switch to NaturallySpeaking Switch to NatSpeak	make NaturallySpeaking the active program
Switch to <program name>	switch to any open program—"program name" should be the name as it appears in the title bar of the program window

To start a program by voice, say "Start" plus the program name. For example, "Quicken" or "Start Internet Explorer." You can say any program name that appears in the Windows Start menu.

Use the same command, "Start," to open programs on the Windows desktop, folders, and documents in the start menu. Say "Start" plus the name of the program, folder, or document. For documents, be sure to spell out the whole document name. To open "readme.txt," say "Start read me dot t x t."

Pressing Keys by Voice

All Windows menus and controls can be activated by pressing keys. This section explains how to press any key by voice.

Letters

To type a key, say "Press" plus the name of the key you want. Instead of "Press" you can also say "Type" or "Press Key."

- ▶ For letters, say the name of the letter ("Press k").
- ▶ For capital letters, say "Cap" plus the letter ("Press Cap k").
- ▶ For better accuracy with letters, use the radio alphabet ("Press kilo").

The radio alphabet:

alpha	golf	Mike	Sierra	Yankee
bravo	hotel	November	tango	Zulu
Charlie	India	Oscar	uniform	
delta	Juliet	papa	Victor	
echo	kilo	Quebec	whiskey	
foxtrot	Lima	Romeo	x-ray	

The command "Scratch That" does not work after using "Press"—it will not undo a keypress command.

Punctuation

For punctuation and special characters, say the name ("Press percent sign"). See the punctuation table on page 77.

The most useful keys	The others
Space Bar	Caps Lock
Tab Key	Print Screen
Enter Key	Scroll Lock
Escape Key	Pause Key
Backspace Key	Num Lock
Delete Key	Home Key
Page Up	End Key
Page Down	Insert Key
Up Arrow	Function 1 *or* F1 *to*
Down Arrow	Function 12 *or* F12
Left Arrow	Keypad 1 *to* Keypad 9
Right Arrow	Keypad period, Keypad slash, Keypad minus, Keypad plus, Keypad Enter

Modifiers

The modifier keys are "Alt Key," "Control Key," and "Shift Key." Or say them without the word "key"—"Alt," "Control," and "Shift." You must say them along with the key they modify. Some examples:

Say any of these	To do this
Press Control papa Press Control Key papa Press Control p Type Control p	press Ctrl+P, the Print command (in most programs)
Press Shift Tab Press Shift Key Tab Key	backtab
Press Alt f (pause) Press a	choose the Save As command, in most programs (open the File menu, then pick Save As)
Press Control Key Alt Key 1 Press Control Alt 1	select Heading 1 style in Microsoft Word

Activating Commands by Saying Key Names

Menus

All menus and almost all dialog box controls have one letter underlined. To open a menu, say "Press Alt" plus the underlined letter. Once the menu is open, say the underlined letter in the command you want (there's no need to say "Alt" first). To choose Print Preview in NaturallySpeaking, for example, say "Press Alt f (pause) Press v."

Dialog Boxes

To activate a dialog box control, say "Press Alt" plus the underlined letter of the control. In Figure 9-2, say "Press Alt p" for the Properties button, "Press Alt o" for the Collate checkbox, and so on. "Press Enter" will choose whichever button has a bold border (in Figure 9-2, the OK button). "Press Escape" will choose the Cancel button.

Figure 9-2

Each control in a Windows dialog box has one letter underlined (shown with an arrow in the diagram). Say "Press Alt" plus the underlined letter to activate that control. To check the Collate checkbox, for example, say "Press Alt o."

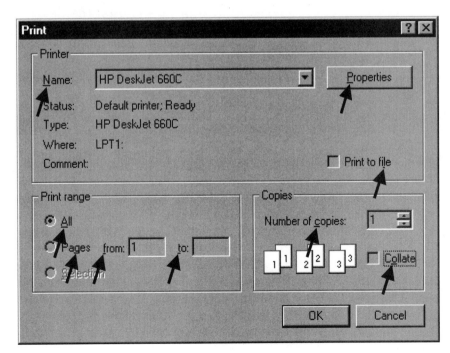

You can also activate a control by selecting it and pressing the space bar. To select each control of a dialog box in turn, press the Tab key ("Press Tab" or "Press Tab Key"). To move in reverse, press Shift plus Tab ("Press Shift Tab"). As you move, the control selected will have a thin dotted line around it. (In Figure 9-2, the selected control is Collate.) Say "press space bar" to activate the selected control (to check the checkbox or push the button).

Some dialog boxes are organized by graphical tabs (Figure 9-3). To move from one tab to the next, press Ctrl plus Tab. To move to the previous tab, press Ctrl plus Shift plus Tab. Say "Press Control Tab" and "Press Control Shift Tab."

Figure 9-3
The tabs in a tabbed dialog box.

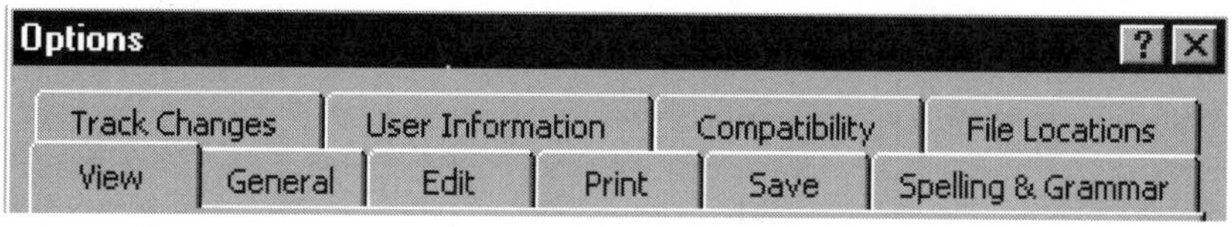

Arrow Keys

The voice commands for pressing arrow keys are essential for navigating within lists and on the desktop. Say "Move Up 1" to "Move Up 20" (any number from 1 to 20). This works for all four directions:

- ▶ "Move Down 1" to "Move Down 20"
- ▶ "Move Up 1" to "Move Up 20"
- ▶ "Move Left 1" to "Move Left 20"
- ▶ "Move Right 1" to "Move Right 20"

Using Online Help by Voice

Say "Give Me Help" to open NaturallySpeaking's online help. The same dialog box commands discussed above work here. Move to different topics with "Move Up 3" and "Move Down 3" (use any number from 1 to 20). To open a topic, say "Press Enter." To choose tabs or buttons, say "Click" plus the name ("Click Find," "Click Display").

Mouse by Voice

Clicks and Drags

To click the mouse by voice, move the pointer where you want it, and say one of these commands.

Say this	To do this
Mouse Click Mouse Left-Click	click the left mouse button
Mouse Right-Click	click the right mouse button
Mouse Double-Click	double-click the left mouse button
Mouse Mark	remember this point as the beginning point of a mouse drag
Mouse Drag	drag the mouse from the "mark" point to here

To drag from one point to another, move to the start point and say "Mouse Mark." Then move to the end point and say "Mouse Drag." To practice with these commands, drag icons on the Windows desktop or drag the paintbrush in Paint.

If clicking the mouse button is uncomfortable for you, try moving the mouse by hand but clicking it by voice using these commands.

Mouse Movements

Say "Mouse" plus a direction (up, down, left, right) plus the number of units to move (1 to 10). Examples: "Mouse Up 7," "Mouse Left 3." Each unit is a few pixels on the screen.

MouseGrid

Use the MouseGrid commands to move the mouse pointer longer distances. First, move the pointer where you want it:

- ▶ Say "MouseGrid." A numbered grid appears.
- ▶ Say the number closest to where you want the mouse to go. The grid will be redrawn smaller.
- ▶ Say more numbers until the mouse pointer is where you want it. If you make a mistake, say "Undo That" to go back.

Second, say one of these mouse commands:

▶ Click (same as Left Click)
▶ Double-Click
▶ Left-Click
▶ Right-Click
▶ Mark (at the beginning point of a mouse drag)
▶ Drag (at the end point of a mouse drag)

To drag from one point to the other, use the MouseGrid to move to the start point, and say "Mark." Then use the MouseGrid to move to the end point, and say "Drag."

You can combine MouseGrid commands without pausing ("MouseGrid 9 1 Click").

To cancel the MouseGrid, say "Cancel."

Hands-Free Tips

Here are some more tips on how to best work by voice if you have limited hand use.

▶ The command "Start" starts programs and documents that are at any level of the Windows Start menu.

▶ If you have no or minimal hand use, set NaturallySpeaking so that the microphone is on (sleeping) when the program starts. For instructions on how to do this, see page 217.

▶ To open a window's control menu, so you can close, minimize, or resize the window, say "Click Control Menu." This command can be a useful alternative if NaturallySpeaking is not recognizing "Click Close" and other window control commands.

▶ To move around the Start menu, the Windows desktop, and many other parts of the computer, use the "Move" commands. You can say "Move Up 4," for example, which acts like pressing the up-arrow key four times. You can say "Move Up," "Move Down," "Move Right," and "Move Left," plus a number 1 to 20. You must say a number to make this command work.

▶ In the Windows Start menu, the "Move" commands are the easiest way to activate Shut Down, Logoff, Help, Run, Find, and Settings. For example, to use Find, Say "Click Start," "Move Up 5," then "Press Enter Key" (on most computers, Find is the fifth item from the bottom of the Start Menu).

10

Automate Your Work

One of the most exciting features of NaturallySpeaking is its ability to automate your work. Instead of typing the 50 characters of your street address, for example, you can just say "address line." To start a new e-mail message addressed to Jackie, just say "New Message for Jackie."

Using voice shorthands, forms, and macros will make your work more efficient. With shorthands, you can say one thing ("work phone number") and NaturallySpeaking will type something else ("510-555-9435"). Macros, discussed in Chapter 11, are more powerful than shorthands. Macros can type large passages of text and execute computer commands. Forms, described at the end of this chapter, let you complete reports and correspondence more quickly.

Shorthands:

> ▶ are available in all editions of NaturallySpeaking.
> ▶ can type up to 126 characters with one voice command.
> ▶ cannot exceed one line (no carriage returns).
> ▶ cannot contain tabs, modifier keys, or other nonprinting characters.
> ▶ cannot contain backslashes.

Macros:

> ▶ are available only in the Professional, Medical, and Legal editions of NaturallySpeaking.
> ▶ can type any amount of text with one voice command, up to 16,000 characters.
> ▶ can execute computer commands, such as checking e-mail or clicking the mouse.
> ▶ can include variables ("send e-mail to <name>").

In the Professional, Medical, and Legal editions, one user can have separate vocabularies for dictating on different topics. Shorthands are stored separately within each vocabulary. Macros, however, are specific to the user and shared across all vocabularies.

If you'd like to use macros and your edition of Naturally-Speaking does not include them, upgrades are available. See Chapter 20 for more information.

Which to Use—Shorthand or Macro?

If you want to type text that's all on one line and less than 126 characters, use a shorthand. While a macro can do the same thing, shorthands do not require a pause before and after you say them, making them easier to use in dictation.

Creating Shorthands

To create a shorthand, decide:

> ▶ the shorthand's name, which is what you will say to the computer.
> ▶ what you want the computer to type.

Choose a name that's more than one word long and that's not something you would typically use in dictation. The name plus what the shorthand types can be up to 126 characters combined.

Bad Names and Good Names

Bad shorthand names are those you'd often say while dictating, such as phone, phone number, my phone number, and e-mail address. You might dictate a sentence about phones and find out your phone number has popped up in the middle of it.

Good shorthand names are unusual enough that you'd rarely say them while dictating. You might end frequently used shorthands with the word "line." This makes the shorthand names unique, but easy to remember. Also, NaturallySpeaking recognizes longer names (three syllables or more) more accurately than shorter names.

> ▶ Examples of good names (there are many): phone number line, e-mail address line

To create a shorthand name that includes letters spoken separately, separate the letters with spaces to make it easier for NaturallySpeaking to recognize the pronunciation.

> ▶ Example: In the Spoken Form box, type "U F O," not "UFO."

If you want the computer to type the name of a shorthand instead of the shorthand itself, pause briefly in the middle of saying the name, then continue. Pause between words, not in the middle of a word.

Making a New Shorthand

From the Tools menu in NaturallySpeaking, choose Vocabulary Editor. The Vocabulary Editor window appears. This window shows all the words in your active vocabulary, in alphabetical order (Figure 10-1).

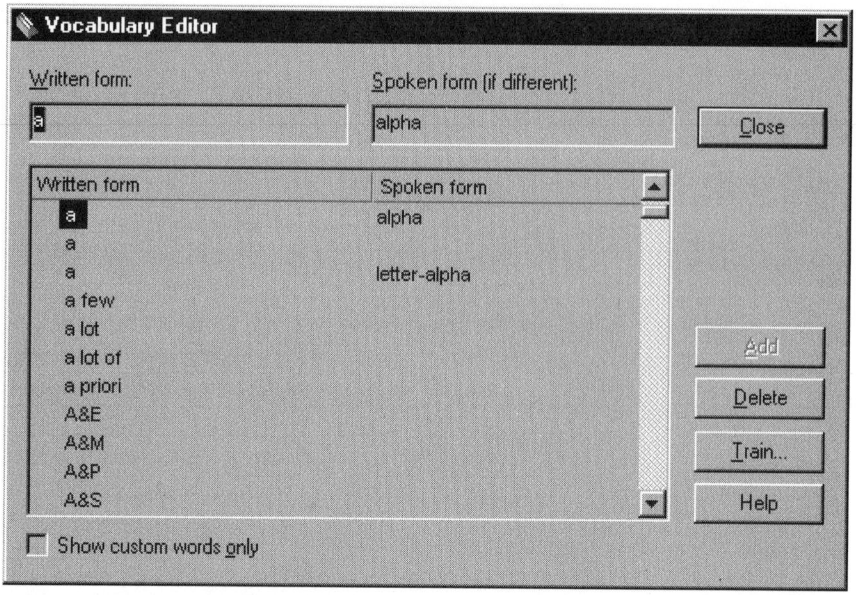

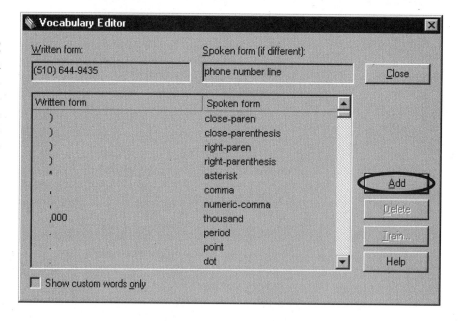

Figure 10-1
The Vocabulary
Editor.

Figure 10-2
Creating a
shorthand.
Type the written
form and spoken
form, then click
Add.

Most words are typed the same way they're spoken. In Figure 10-1 above, "A&P" and "a priori" are this way. A few words are spoken differently than they are typed. Saying "alpha" types the letter "a." So does saying "letter-alpha." Both are dictation shorthands already built into NaturallySpeaking.

To create your own shorthand, type the spoken form (the shorthand's name) on the right and the written form (what the computer should type) on the left. Then click the Add button to add the new shorthand to your vocabulary (Figure 10-2).

Like all added words and shorthands, your new shorthand will have a large red asterisk to its left (Figure 10-3). Click the Train button to pronounce the shorthand once and teach the computer how you say it.

Figure 10-3

Click Train to teach the computer how you say the shorthand name.

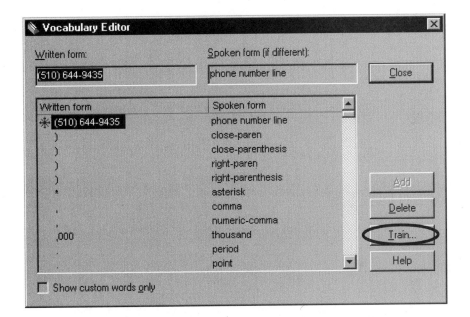

Click the Close button when you're done creating shorthands. Save your speech files (click the Save Speech Files button on the NaturallySpeaking toolbar), then test your shorthands to be sure they work.

If a shorthand doesn't work, check for the most common shorthand mistakes:

▸ the spoken form and written form were reversed.
▸ you forgot to click Add after entering the spoken and written forms.

If things are as they should be, try training the shorthand again. Choose Vocabulary Editor from the Tools menu, click on the word, and click the Train button.

Sometimes, for no apparent reason, a shorthand just won't work. Change the shorthand's name, train the new name, and try again—this often solves the problem.

Changing Shorthands

To change a shorthand, open the Vocabulary Editor (choose Vocabulary Editor from the NaturallySpeaking Tools menu). Find the shorthand you want by typing the first few letters of the shorthand's written form in the Written Form box. Select the shorthand, then edit the written form and spoken form as desired. Click Add to add the new word. This adds a new shorthand—it does not replace the shorthand you modified. Find the old shorthand, click on it to select it, and click Delete. If your new shorthand has a new spoken form, be sure to train it. Select the new shorthand and click Train.

Shorthand Ideas

Voice shorthands are much easier to remember than keyboard macros, and you can create several thousand of them if you are that ambitious. It's well worth the time to create shorthands for any repetitive text that is longer than a few words or that includes numbers or punctuation. Substitute your own contact information for the examples below.

You say	The computer types
phone number line	(510) 555-9435
e-mail address line	sales@SayICan.com
Web site line	http://www.SayICan.com

The shorthand names in these next two examples are rarely used in dictation, so there's no need to make them more distinct by adding "line" or some other word.

company name	Say I Can
Yahoo address	www.yahoo.com

Create synonyms to make your life easier. Synonyms are shorthands that have different names but that all type the same text. Our brains are built to remember meaning, not exact wording, so creating several versions of the same shorthand makes using shorthands more natural.

You say	The computer types
phone number line my phone line print phone number print work phone phone shorthand	(510) 644-9435

Shorthands also work well for phrases with unusual capitalization, such as institutions, organizations, or titles. You can have the shorthand be short for a longer phrase:

UC Berkeley	University of California at Berkeley
I B S long (not "I B S" by itself, because you may sometimes want to type just the acronym by saying IBS)	International Bureau of Standards

You can put the whole phrase in as a shorthand (actually, you're adding a new word). You say the whole phrase, but it will be capitalized correctly each time.

international bureau of standards	International Bureau of Standards
the catcher in the rye	The Catcher in the Rye

Without the shorthand, you'd have to say the capitalization manually.

Cap international Cap bureau of Cap standards	International Bureau of Standards
Cap the Cap catcher in the Cap rye	The Catcher in the Rye

Shorthands are the best way to speak words with accented characters. Type the word with accented characters in your word processor, copy it, switch to the Vocabulary Editor (Figure 10-2), and paste it into the Written Form box.

Spoken form	Written form
attache	attaché
manana	mañana

Shorthands are perfect for passages you use repeatedly.

You say	The computer types
personal thank you	It was a pleasure speaking with you today about our products. Please call as other questions may arise.
phone sentence	My phone number is (510) 555-9435.

Shorthands cannot print text that includes a line break, such as an address. Use a macro instead, if your edition of Naturally-Speaking allows it.

To work around this limitation, you can create several shorthands:

Spoken form	Written form
first address	Say I Can
second address	2039 Shattuck Ave. Suite 500
third address	Berkeley, CA 94704

Say them in sequence:

You say	The computer types
first address New Line second address New Line third address	Say I Can 2039 Shattuck Ave. Suite 500 Berkeley, CA 94704

Filling in Forms by Voice

Like shorthands, voice-activated forms let you avoid dictating the same text repeatedly. These forms work like paper forms. The structure and body of your document are already there—just fill in the blanks.

To create a form, first create a document in Word or WordPerfect and put this text wherever there would be a "blank" in the form: NEXT FIELD 1, NEXT FIELD 2, etc. Number each blank consecutively. Your document might look like this:

Dear NEXT FIELD 1,

This letter is to confirm your appointment on NEXT FIELD 2 for a demonstration of NEXT FIELD 3. I look forward to seeing you then.

Save the form as a template. When you want to use this form, open the template and say "Select next field 1." The text "Next Field 1" will be selected. Then dictate the client's name—it will replace the selection. Say "Select next field 2," then dictate the date. Say "select next field 3" to continue. When you're finished, save the new document under a new name (the client's name, perhaps) and print it.

The forms method described here is simple to use and reliable. You can create more complex forms with the template features of your word processor and custom NaturallySpeaking macros, though instructions for this are beyond the scope of this book.

11

Macros

Macros are the more powerful cousin of the shorthands described in Chapter 10. While shorthands are limited to typing short passages of text, macros can type passages as long as you like and also execute computer commands. Consult Chapter 10 to see whether a shorthand or a macro is best for your needs.

This book uses the term "macro" for what the Naturally-Speaking documentation calls a "command," to distinguish between commands you create yourself (macros) and commands built in to the computer ("Scratch That" and many more). Technically, however, when you create a macro you're actually creating a new command that NaturallySpeaking treats just like built-in commands.

As described in the previous chapter, macros:

▶ can type any amount of text with one voice command, up to 16,000 characters.

▶ can execute computer commands, such as checking e-mail or clicking the mouse.

▶ can include variables ("send e-mail to <name>").

▶ are available only in the Professional, Medical, and Legal editions of NaturallySpeaking.

In the Professional, Medical, and Legal editions, one user can have several vocabularies for dictating on different topics. While shorthands are stored separately within each vocabulary, macros are shared across all vocabularies for a specific user.

If you'd like to use macros but your edition of Naturally-Speaking does not include them, upgrades are available. See Chapter 20 for more information.

Creating Macros

To make a macro, first decide what you want your macro to do. Here are the options:

▶ Type text. For example, your macro can type an address, the signature block in a letter, or three pages of special clauses in a contract.

▶ Execute a computer command. For example, your macro can display the Print Preview window or send an e-mail message.

Second, decide what to name your macro. Unlike shorthand names, it is fine for macro names to be the same phrases that you would typically use in dictation, such as "my address." This works because when you say a macro, you pause before and after saying it. The pauses let the computer know that you want to use the macro, not type its name.

You say	The computer types
my address is in the directory period	My address is in the directory.
(pause) My Address (pause) is in the directory period	3145 Main Street Circleville, FL 10022 is in the directory.

Capitalize each word of your macro name to distinguish it from regular dictation when it's necessary to correct it in the Correction window.

Third, decide whether you want the macro to be available in all programs or just in one application. Macros that type text are typically useful in all programs—they should be "global." Macros that execute a command should be only available in the one program where the command works ("application-specific").

Tutorial: A Macro That Types Text

In this step-by-step tutorial, you'll create the macro "My Address," which types an address. From the NaturallySpeaking Tools menu, choose New Command Wizard (Figure 11-1).

Figure 11-1
Is the macro useful in just one program, or everywhere?

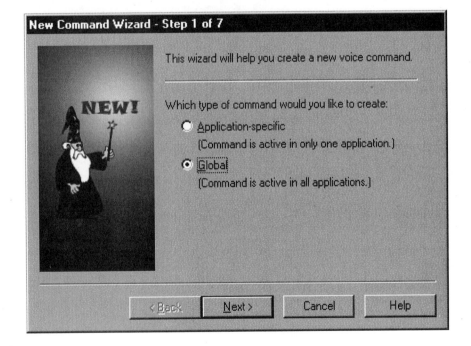

This macro will be useful in all programs, so select Global. Click the Next button—NaturallySpeaking skips right to "Step 4 of 7" (Figure 11-2). Type the macro name and click Next.

Figure 11-2
Type the command name (macro name) and click Next.

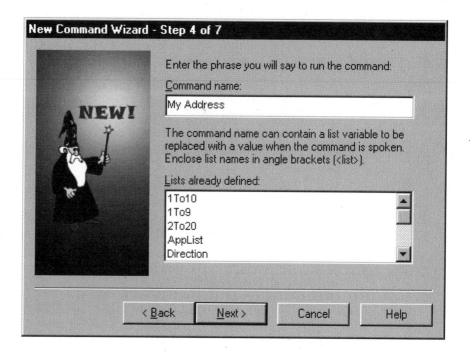

Figure 11-3
This macro will type text.

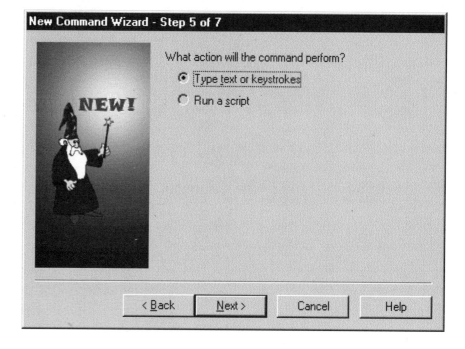

This sample macro will type text. Select the Type Text or Keystrokes button and click Next (Figure 11-3).

Type the text of the address (Figure 11-4). Leave a blank line after it (press Enter after the zip code) so that when Naturally-Speaking types the text it will automatically move on to the next line.

Instead of typing, you can copy text from your document, then paste it into this window by pressing Ctrl+V. This is especially useful for long passages.

Figure 11-4

Type your address.

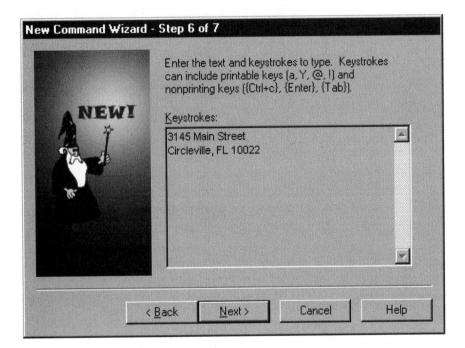

Click Next, review the information, and click Finish (Figure 11-5). If you find an error, use the Back button to go back and fix it.

Now, when you say "My Address," NaturallySpeaking will type the address you entered (Figure 11-6). Remember to pause before and after saying it.

Figure 11-5
Double-check the
information,
then press
Finish.

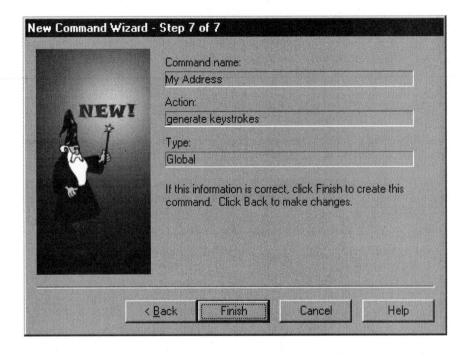

Figure 11-6
Say "My Address."
It works! You'll
never have to type
your address again.

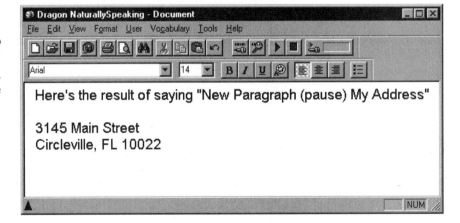

Tutorial: A Macro That Executes a Command

In this second tutorial, you'll create the macro "New Message," which starts a new e-mail message. This macro is meant to work only in Eudora—it's application-specific. In Eudora, the keystrokes to make a new message are Ctrl+N. Your new macro will have NaturallySpeaking send those keys to Eudora whenever you say "New Message." Eudora will think you actually typed Ctrl+N and it will open a new message window.

If you don't use Eudora, you can write this macro to work with any e-mail program. Start your e-mail program, find the key sequence that creates a new message, and use that sequence in place of Ctrl+N in this example.

To begin, be sure Eudora or your e-mail program is open. From the NaturallySpeaking Tools menu, choose New Command Wizard. Choose Application-specific and click Next. The next screen shows a list of all open programs (Figure 11-7).

Figure 11-7
Choose the program this macro will operate in, then click Next.

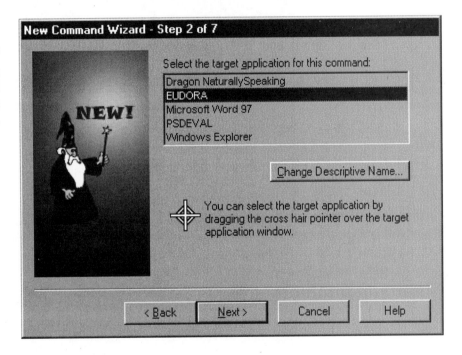

The next window, "Step 3 of 7" (Figure 11-8), shows a list of subwindows ("target windows" or dialog boxes) active in the main program. In this example, there's only one choice, "Eudora Pro." Click to select it, then click Next.

If there's more than one subwindow in this list, choosing the name of the program is usually best. You may have to test your macro with several subwindows to see which works.

Figure 11-8
In this case, there's only one target window to choose from.

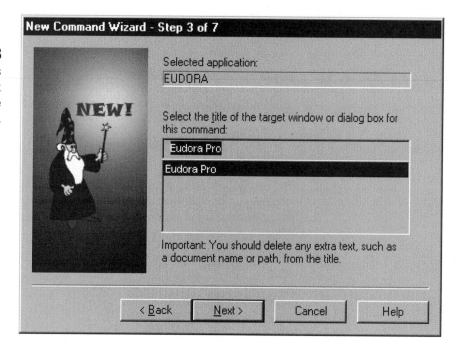

In "Step 4 of 7" (Figure 11-9), type the macro name and click Next.

Figure 11-9
Type the macro name.

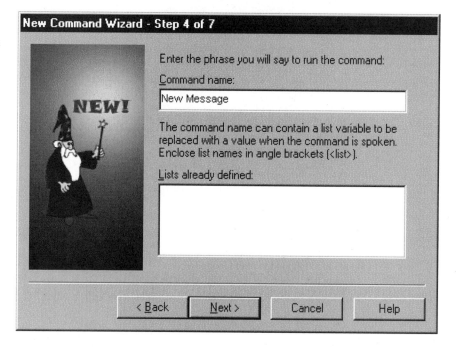

On the next screen, "Step 5 of 7" (not shown), select Type Text or Keystrokes and click Next.

In Step 6 (Figure 11-10), enter the keystrokes to be typed. In this example, type {Ctrl+n} as shown. Be sure the "n" is lowercase. Do not press Enter afterward—this macro should not include a carriage return (blank line). (For key codes besides Ctrl+N, see Macro Key Codes, below.) Click Next to continue.

Figure 11-10
Enter the keys, or key codes, this macro should type.

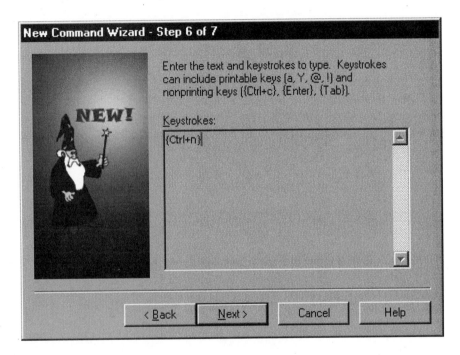

In Step 7 (not shown), double-check the information listed and click Finish.

Macro Key Codes

To have your keystroke macro type a letter or punctuation mark, just type the letter or punctuation mark (no brackets needed). For other keys, use these codes:

The Most Useful Macro Key Codes

To type this	Enter this
Alt	{Alt}
Backspace	{BackSpace}
Control	{Ctrl}
Del	{Del}
Down Arrow	{Down}
End	{End}
Enter	{Enter}
Home	{Home}
Left Arrow	{Left}
Right Arrow	{Right}
Shift	{Shift}
Space	{Space}
Tab	{Tab}
Up Arrow	{Up}

Other Codes

Caps Lock	{CapsLock}
Break	{Break} (must be preceded by {Ctrl})
Center	{Center} (this is numeric keypad key 5 when NumLock is off)
Esc	{Esc}
Function Keys: F1, F2,...F16	{F1}, {F2},...{F16}
Insert	{Ins}
Num Lock	{NumLock} (extended keyboards only)
Numeric keypad keys (handled as if NumLock is on)	{NumKey0}, {NumKey1},...{NumKey9}, {NumKey.}, {NumKey*}, {NumKey-}, {NumKey+}
Page Down	{PgDn}
Page Up	{PgUp}
Pause	{Pause}
Print Screen	{Prtsc}
Scroll Lock	{ScrollLock}
Sys Req	{SysReq}

Modifier Keys

The "modifier keys"—Alt, Ctrl, and Shift—are usually pressed at the same time as a letter. To indicate this, put a plus sign after the key name, followed by the letter. Use the lowercase letter.

▶ Example: {Alt+e} presses Alt and "e" together. In most programs, this opens the Edit menu.

Use the uppercase letter only if you want the Shifted version of that key.

▶ Example: {Alt+N} is handled like pressing three keys at once—Alt, Shift and "n."

For several modifier keys at once, separate the keys by plus signs.

▶ Example: {Ctrl+Alt+t}

In a few rare programs the left and right modifier keys act differently. In this case (if it's necessary to specify which of the two Shift, Ctrl, or Alt keys to use) type {LeftShift} or {RightShift}, {LeftCtrl} or {RightCtrl}, and {LeftAlt} or {RightAlt}.

Save, Train, and Test

After creating a macro, save your speech files (click the Save Speech Files button on the NaturallySpeaking toolbar). This is especially important if you intend your macro to do more than just type text.

Before testing a macro, save your speech files! If the macro causes a program error, you won't have to recreate the macro from scratch.

Next, train each macro. This step is optional but recommended. From the NaturallySpeaking Tools menu, choose Train Words. Type the new macro name exactly as you created it and click OK (Figure 11-11).

Figure 11-11
Type the macro
name and click OK.

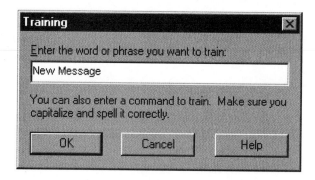

The Train Words window will appear (Figure 11-12).

Figure 11-12
Say the macro
name to teach
NaturallySpeaking
how you
pronounce it.

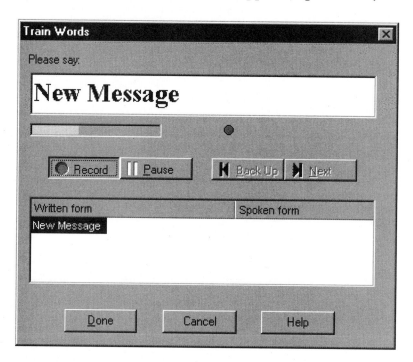

Click Record, then say the macro name. Then click Done.
Now say the macro to be sure that it works. If it doesn't work:

▶ Remember to pause before and after saying the macro.
▶ Try training it again.
▶ Be sure you're in the right application (for an application-specific macro).

If the macro still doesn't work, see Macro Troubleshooting, page 258.

Changing a Macro

To modify a macro after it's created, choose Edit Command Wizard from the NaturallySpeaking Tools menu. Choose whether your macro is application-specific or global, and click Next.

If your macro is global, choose the macro you want to edit from the list of available commands (Figure 11-13). Click Next, type a new name for the macro if you wish, and click Next again to edit the macro's text or script. Click Next and then Finish. This process is similar to creating a new macro.

Figure 11-13
Click on the macro
you want to edit.

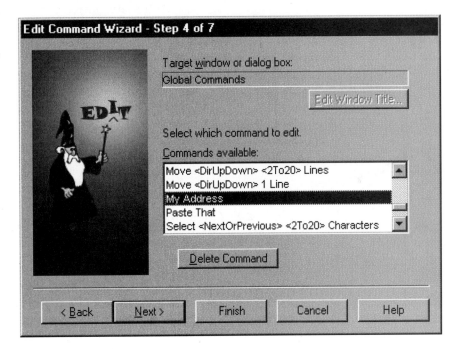

If your macro is application-specific, choose the correct application and click Next. Click on the same target window you selected when you originally created the macro (see Figure 11-8). Click Next. In Step 4, choose the macro you want to edit from the list of available commands (Figure 11-13). Click Next, type a new name for the macro if you wish, and click Next again to edit the macro's text or script. Click Next and then Finish.

Unfortunately, there's no way to change the target window of a macro once it's been created. If you need to change the target window on your macro, recreate the macro with New Command Wizard.

Sending Keystrokes

The macros in the tutorials above do quite different things. One types text that's used frequently. The other executes a command—it instructs the computer to start a new e-mail message.

To NaturallySpeaking, however, these two macros work in the same way. Each sends keystrokes to the active program, fooling it into thinking that you are typing.

The easiest way to create macros is to send keystrokes, as in these two examples. Even formatted text and menu commands can be entered just by typing the correct keys. Try typing the keystrokes yourself, by hand, to verify that they really do work. Try these examples in WordPad or the NaturallySpeaking window.

To get this	Type this
Who knows *what* will happen next?	Who knows {Ctrl+i}what{Ctrl+i} will happen next? (The {Ctrl+i} key combination turns on and off italics in most word processing programs.)
Jan. Feb. Mar.	Jan.{Tab}Feb.{Tab}Mar.
open Find dialog box	{Ctrl+f}
open Find dialog box (alternate method)	{Alt+e}f (Type Alt and "e" together. This opens the Edit menu. Then press "f" to choose Find.)
print preview	{Alt+f}v
minimize the window	{Alt+Space}n
select to end of line	{Shift+End}
go to end of document and type "Created by A.K."	{Ctrl+End}{Enter}Created by A.K.

Windows Keyboard Shortcuts

To create the type of macro that send keystrokes, it's useful to first review the kinds of actions available from keyboard shortcuts. Keyboard shortcuts work the same in all Windows programs.

> ▶ Common menu commands have shortcut keys assigned already. Find the command you want and check if a shortcut key already exists (Figure 11-14).

Figure 11-14
In this menu, four commands have built-in shortcuts. The arrow indicates the shortcut for Save, "Ctrl+S."

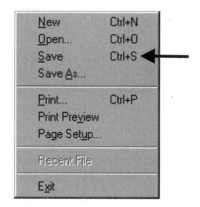

> ▶ All menu names have an underlined letter. To open a menu by keyboard, press Alt plus the underlined letter (Figure 11-15).

Figure 11-15
Every menu name in every Windows program has an underlined letter.

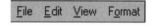

> ▶ Once a menu is open, all commands on the menu also have an underlined letter. (In Figure 11-14, for example, the letter for Print Preview is "v.") Press the underlined letter to choose the command. (Don't press Alt again—just press the letter.)
> ▶ Dialog boxes are the small windows that open when you choose a menu command with three dots after it ("Print...") See Figure 9-2 on page 91 for an example. When a dialog

box is open, use the following key combinations as alternatives to the mouse:

▶ Navigate to or change controls inside a dialog box by pressing Alt plus the underlined letter of the control that you want. (Controls are the buttons, check boxes, menus, and fields in a dialog box.)

▶ To move through every control shown, press Tab repeatedly. When the command you want is selected, it will be enclosed by a small dotted rectangle. Press the space bar or Enter to execute the command.

▶ To move through every control in reverse, press Shift plus Tab.

▶ To click the button with a bold border, press the space bar or Enter. Usually the bold bolder encircles the OK button.

▶ To click the Cancel button, which every dialog box has, press Esc.

Some computer commands cannot be executed by pressing keys. For example, there's no way to click the mouse by keyboard. There's also no way to create a keystroke macro "Erase Now" to do the same thing as the built-in command "Scratch That." Both these macros must be created using NaturallySpeaking's scripting commands, described in "Script Macros" below. Most useful macros, however, can be created by sending keystrokes, and keystroke macros are much easier than script macros to create and test. Use keystroke macros whenever possible.

Step-by-Step: Creating a Keystroke Macro

1. Write down on paper the sequence of keys your macro will press.
2. Test the key sequence manually. Type the keys just as you have them written down, to make sure that they work.
3. To create a new macro:

   ▶ Choose New Command Wizard (Tools menu in NaturallySpeaking).

▶ Choose Application-specific or Global, as desired. (If the macro is application-specific, also choose the appropriate application and target window.)
▶ Enter the macro name.
▶ Choose the Type Text or Keystrokes button.
▶ Enter the key sequence from your notes.
▶ Choose Finish.

4. Save your speech files.
5. Train the macro.
6. Test it: say the macro name and watch what happens.

Script Macros

NaturallySpeaking includes a scripting language, a tool for creating macros that do things you can't do by just typing keys. With script macros, you can create voice macros that:

▶ click the mouse.
▶ mimic a built-in NaturallySpeaking command.
▶ include a variable ("new message to <name>," where <name> might be any of 40 different people).

The NaturallySpeaking scripting language is complex and powerful. This book presents some useful script macros and discusses just a few of the twenty-plus scripting commands. For further information on scripts, see the topic "Scripting Language Reference" in the NaturallySpeaking online help. Also review Dragon Systems' 100+ page manual *Creating Voice Commands,* available as a free download from www.dragonsys.com.

Tutorial: Creating a Script Macro

This example demonstrates how to create a macro called "Erase That Phrase." The macro will have the same effect as saying "Scratch That"—it's a synonym to that command. Creating synonyms can make using NaturallySpeaking easier because you can say either command—you don't have to remember a command name that's built in. This macro will be Global— available in all programs.

Creating a script macro begins like creating a macro that presses keys. Choose New Command Wizard from the Naturally-Speaking tools menu. Choose Global and click Next (as in Figure

11-1). Type the macro name "Erase That Phrase" and click Next. This brings up the window "Step 5 of 7" (Figure 11-16). Choose the Run a Script button and click Next.

Figure 11-16
This will be a script macro.

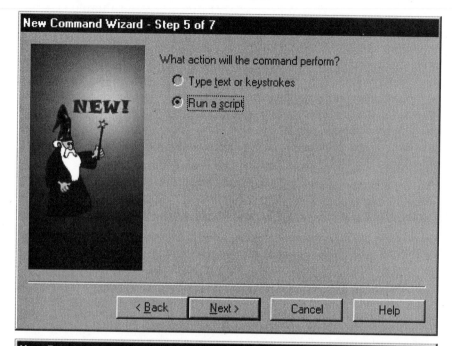

Figure 11-17
The script for this command is:
HeardWord "Scratch","That"

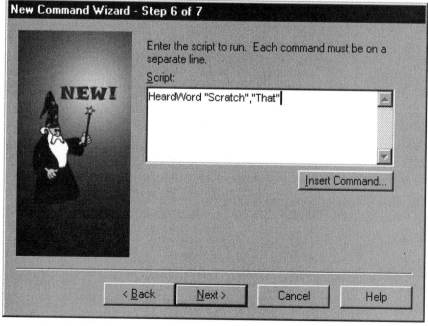

Enter the script to run in the Script window (Figure 11-17). In this example, type the HeardWord command exactly as shown, with no spaces.

Click Next, then Finish to complete this script macro. Now save your speech files, train the macro, and test it. When you say "Erase That Phrase," the computer should act as if you said "Scratch That."

The script command HeardWord is a special instruction to NaturallySpeaking. It tells NaturallySpeaking to act as if it heard the words in the command.

The script for this sample macro had only one command. However, script macros can include any number of commands (up to 16,000 characters total). Each script command must go on a separate line.

Selected Script Commands

These script commands are among the most useful.

HeardWord

HeardWord makes NaturallySpeaking act as if you said a particular word or phrase. Each HeardWord command can include up to eight words. NaturallySpeaking acts as if they were all said together in the same phrase.

The HeardWord command lets you easily create synonyms for existing commands, making them easier to remember. You might, as in the example, create a macro "Erase That Phrase" to do the same thing as "Scratch That." You could then say whichever one came to mind first. Similarly, the macro "Make It Small" could be created as a synonym to Minimize. The scripts for these two macros are:

HeardWord "Scratch","That"	acts as if you said Scratch That
HeardWord "Minimize"	acts as if you said Minimize

The HeardWord command allows the easy creation of more complex, multi-step macros. This two-line macro selects the previous paragraph and makes it bold.

```
HeardWord "Select","Last","Paragraph"
HeardWord "Bold","That"
```

Planning and testing are the secrets of creating macros with HeardWord. Test the commands first by speaking them (say "Select Last Paragraph," (pause) "Bold That"). Create a script for these commands only after you're sure they have the effect you desire.

SendKeys

This command types the keystrokes you specify. It's especially useful when you want to send keystrokes and use other scripting commands in the same macro. If all your macro does is send keystrokes, a keystroke macro is usually sufficient—a script is not needed.

The key codes for these commands are the same as for keystroke macros (see page 113).

SendKeys "{Ctrl+s}"	presses Ctrl and "s" keys together
SendKeys "Dictated by C.D.{Enter}" types the text indicated	

ButtonClick

This command sends mouse clicks. Including numbers after the command indicates which mouse button is pressed and how many times.

This command	*Does this*
ButtonClick	click the left mouse button once
ButtonClick 1,2	click the left mouse button twice
ButtonClick 2,1	click the right mouse button once

Using Lists

Lists allow you to write one macro that can take many forms. Macros of this type have part of the macro name that changes. The part that changes is called a variable. All the possible values for the variable are specified by you in a list.

Here's an example that creates a new e-mail message addressed to any of four people on a name list. This macro is called "New Message to <name>."

The possible names in this example are Ben Franklin, Thomas Jefferson, George Washington, and Abraham Lincoln. To use this macro, you'll say "New Message to Ben Franklin," "New Message to Thomas Jefferson," and so on.

This example is written for Eudora Pro 4.0. You can customize it easily to your own e-mail software. Substitute your software's "new message" keys for Ctrl+N, and substitute your own friends' names for the founding fathers.

To begin, choose New Command Wizard from the Naturally-Speaking Tools menu. Create an application-specific macro for your e-mail program. Name the macro "New Message to <name>" and include the angle brackets ("<", ">") but not the quotes (see Figure 11-18).

Click Next, choose the Run a Script button and click Next again. Enter the following three-line script, as shown in Figure 11-19. (The "_" mark is an underscore character—press Shift plus the hyphen key to type it.)

```
SendKeys "{Ctrl+n}"
SendKeys _arg1
SendKeys "{Tab}"
```

Figure 11-18
The brackets around "name" indicate that it's a variable.

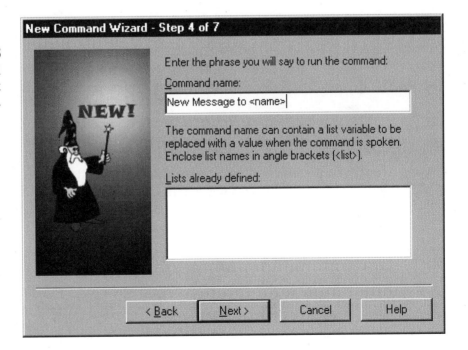

> **New Command Wizard - Step 4 of 7**
>
> NEW!
>
> Enter the phrase you will say to run the command:
>
> Command name:
>
> New Message to <name>
>
> The command name can contain a list variable to be replaced with a value when the command is spoken. Enclose list names in angle brackets (<list>).
>
> Lists already defined:
>
> < Back   Next >   Cancel   Help

Figure 11-19
Type the script shown. Note that NaturallySpeaking assigned the letters "_arg1" to represent the "name" variable.

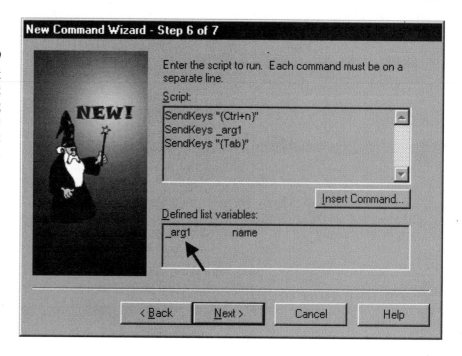

Figure 11-19 includes a box called "Defined list variables," which displays the variable NaturallySpeaking found in your macro name. When you typed in the macro name, the angle brackets signaled to the computer that "name" is actually a variable. NaturallySpeaking assigns the variable its own code, "_arg1."

The script for this macro has three lines. The first line types the Ctrl+N keys, instructing Eudora to start a new e-mail message. The second line, "SendKeys _arg1," types the value of the variable you defined. That is, it types the person's name. The third line types a Tab key, which moves the cursor to the Subject field in the new e-mail message.

Click Next to move to the next screen. Here, type the names you wish to write to. Each name should be on a separate line (Figure 11-20). The names used should match the nicknames in your e-mail program.

Figure 11-20
Type the names of people you regularly e-mail.

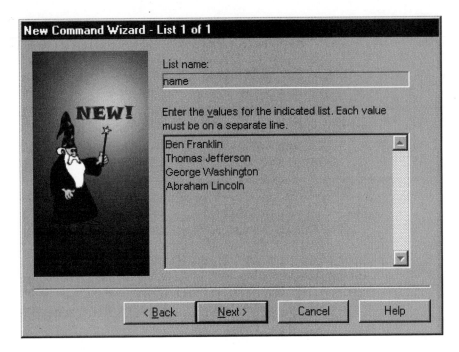

Click Next, then click Finish. Save your speech files and test the macro. (If you wish to train the macro, you need to train each version of it separately: "New Message to George Washington," "New Message to Thomas Jefferson," etc.). Be sure you're in your e-mail program when you test it. The result should be the creation of a new message to the person you said (Figure 11-21).

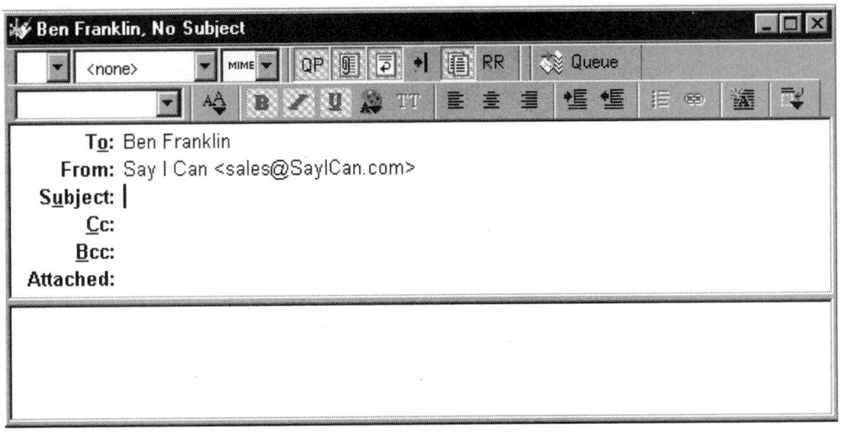

Figure 11-21
The result of saying "New Message to Ben Franklin," a new e-mail message.

To edit a list after it's been created, use Edit Command Wizard. Select the macro involved and click Next until the list appears. You may then edit the list as desired. For example, you could add more names to your names list to make it more useful in sending e-mail.

Macros can have more than one variable in their name and can perform many complex tasks. For more information, see Dragon Systems' manual *Creating Voice Commands*.

Macro Ideas

Macros can improve your efficiency enormously. But don't try to create all possible macros at once. Start with the ones you use most often—perhaps five text macros and a few that execute commands. Keep the name of each macro you make on an index card by your computer as a reminder.

Text Macro Ideas

Each text macro you create saves you from dictating the same thing over and over. Some ideas to get started:

- ▶ Home Address
- ▶ Business Address
- ▶ Address to Laura Raymond (types her address, skips a line, and types "Dear Laura,"). Create these for each person you commonly write to.
- ▶ Signature Block (types "Sincerely yours," skips a line, and types your name)
- ▶ Letter Closing (types a closing paragraph or sentence, then your signature block)
- ▶ Special Offer
- ▶ E-mail Signature (types the signature text for an e-mail message)
- ▶ Address Form (types your name and address, with a Tab after each part of it, for filling in forms on the Web)

More Macro Ideas

Macros that execute commands save you mouse clicks and keystrokes. Start by making voice macros for the commands you use most often.

Many commands can be said by voice without requiring a special macro. Say "click" plus the menu name, then say the command. (Example: say "Click File," then "Print Preview." See Chapter 9 for detailed instructions.) It's easier, however, to write a macro for commands used frequently, so you can say just "Print Preview" as one step.

For All Programs

▶ Create Tab 2 (presses the Tab key twice, for easier navigation in dialog boxes). Also Tab 3, Tab 4, etc.

▶ Create synonyms for commands that are either difficult to remember or are often misrecognized. See the section on scripts, above.

For E-mail

Macro name	Keys in Eudora Pro 4.0	Keys in Lotus Notes 4.5
New Message	{Ctrl+n}	{Alt+c}e
Print Message	{Ctrl+p}	{Ctrl+p}
Send Message	{Ctrl+e}	{Alt+a}e
Read Message	{Enter}	{Enter}
Delete Message	{Ctrl+d}	{Alt+e}l
Reply to Message	{Ctrl+r}	{Alt+c}r
Forward Message	{Alt+m}f	{Alt+a}f
Attach File	{Ctrl+h}	{Alt+f}a

Make up whatever names are easy for you to remember—these are just suggestions. Some people prefer "Message Reply" or "E-mail Back," for example, instead of "Reply to Message."

For Word and WordPerfect

Macro Name	Keys in Word 97	Keys in WordPerfect 8
Today's Date (inserts the date)	{Alt+i}t{Home}{Down} {Down}{Enter}	{Alt+i}d{Enter}
Heading 1 Heading 2 Heading 3 (formats paragraph in heading style one, two, or three)	{Ctrl+Shift+1} {Ctrl+Shift+2} {Ctrl+Shift+3}	

For complex word processing macros, use the word processor's built-in macro feature. Record your macro in Word or WordPerfect and assign it to a keystroke. Then have Naturally-Speaking hit that keystroke. This is the only way to easily create a voice macro that uses Search/Replace and some other word processing functions.

For all programs, start with the ten commands you use most often. Create more commands as you progress.

12

Workflow

As you use NaturallySpeaking, you will develop your own approach to working with the software. Do you dictate first and correct later, or do you correct as you go? Do you use a headset microphone or tape recorder? Do you have an assistant who can edit your dictated documents?

Paying attention to workflow, or how you organize your tasks, is important to maximizing your efficiency with NaturallySpeaking. This chapter suggests ways that people with different needs can manage workflow and increase their productivity.

Dictate First, Correct Later

It's a natural tendency to watch the screen as you dictate and correct the computer's errors as they occur. This is an inefficient way to work, however. Writing takes concentration, and fixing errors as you go can throw you off track.

The best way to work is to dictate anywhere from a few sentences to several paragraphs at once. Then go back and correct any errors the computer has made, while your dictation is still fresh in your mind.

When dictating, you'll achieve higher accuracy and be less distracted if you don't watch the computer. Dictate with your eyes closed. Or look at the ceiling, to the side, or down. Watching the computer as you speak makes your speech rhythms less natural and increases the likelihood of errors.

Listening to Your Recorded Voice

The primary obstacle to dictating first, correcting later is forgetting what you originally said. It's frustrating to discover one of NaturallySpeaking's mistakes but not remember the words you used.

The easiest way to remind yourself of what you said is to listen to your recorded voice. NaturallySpeaking records what you say as you speak in Select-and-Say applications. (In other applications, you can play back only the most recent phrase you said.)

Playing back what you said is easiest if you have the Enable Double-Click to Correct and Automatic Playback on Correction options turned on (see page 217). If these options are on, select NaturallySpeaking's error by double-clicking on it. The Correction window will open, and you'll hear a recording of what you spoke. Click the Play Back button in the Correction window if you want to hear the recording again.

Here are two alternate ways to open the Correction window and hear your speech:

▶ Select the word or words and press "-" (numeric minus key).
▶ Select the word or words and say "Correct That."

These two methods play your speech without opening the Correction window:

▶ Select the word or words and say "Play That Back."

▸ Select the word or words and click on the small red triangle on the NaturallySpeaking toolbar.

Now that you've heard what you originally spoke, correct NaturallySpeaking's error:

▸ If you're in your document, not the Correction window, just type or say the words you want.
▸ If you're in the Correction window, type or spell the words you want only if they *exactly match* the recorded words you just heard. This ensures that the computer will learn your voice correctly.
▸ If you're in the Correction window and you want words different from the recording, close the Correction window (click Close or hit the Esc key). Then type the words you want directly in your document. Do this if any of these is true:

  ▸ you want to edit what you said
  ▸ you originally misspoke, so the recorded sample you heard is not a good basis for teaching the computer
  ▸ you can't understand what you said in the recording
  ▸ there's no recorded audio at all

Listening to the speech NaturallySpeaking records is the easiest and smoothest way to correct. It's simple to select the words that are wrong and press "-" (or say "Correct That") to listen to what you actually said.

The other playback commands besides "Play That Back" are occasionally useful. They are: "Play Back Line," "Play Back Paragraph," "Play Back Document," Play Back Window" (plays just the text in view), "Play Back to Here" (from the top of the window to the cursor) and "Play Back from Here" (from the cursor to the bottom of the window).

While your voice is playing back, you can press the left arrow key to back up, the right arrow key to go faster, and the down arrow key to open the Correction window.

Problems with Recorded Speech Playback

Unfortunately, NaturallySpeaking's speech playback is limited and unreliable. Recorded speech playback is available only in

Select-and-Say applications. Also, you cannot save the sound of your voice along with the document—you have to listen to your speech in the same computer session that it was transcribed.

Even within Select-and-Say applications, playback is often disabled or missing. (The Play Back button in the Correction window will be grayed out and cannot be used.)

Recorded speech playback is most likely to be disabled:

▶ when you're working with text that's been edited
▶ when the surrounding text has been edited

How Audio Playback Works

As you dictate, NaturallySpeaking saves a digital recording of your voice in a file on disk at the same time that it transcribes your words. When you select text on the screen and ask to hear your voice played back, NaturallySpeaking plays the appropriate part of the recording. The program keeps track of what words on the screen correspond to what parts of the file.

In Select-and-Say applications, NaturallySpeaking has full information about what text is on the screen and where the text is located. This lets it find the correct segment to play back in the sound recording file. In other applications, NaturallySpeaking cannot keep track of what's on the screen. It then cannot know what spot in the file to play.

Within Select-and-Say applications, audio playback works pretty well—if you do not edit your text! If little text is moved or changed, NaturallySpeaking is generally successful at keeping track of what text corresponds to what part of the recording file.

However, if you replace some words with others or move a sentence or two, NaturallySpeaking has trouble keeping track of what text on the screen corresponds to what part of the sound file. The frustrating result for the user is no audio playback. It will take some more sophisticated programming to make the audio playback more reliable. Perhaps a future release will make this possible. The ability to save audio playback along with documents would also make using NaturallySpeaking easier.

If Playback Is Unavailable

When NaturallySpeaking will not play back your recorded voice, you still need to figure out what you said so you can correct your text.

Try pronouncing NaturallySpeaking's mistakes out loud. The sound may remind you of what the words were supposed to be.

▶ The program types: "...make sure speech patterns..."
▶ Say it aloud to remember what you said: "...*makes your* speech patterns..."

For complex or difficult dictation that would be hard to reconstruct, have a tape recorder running on your desk as you speak. This serves as a backup record of what you said. It's time-consuming to go back and listen to the whole tape, but it's reassuring to know it's there if needed.

If you have an assistant, he or she can listen to the tape and correct NaturallySpeaking's transcription for you. See the discussion on working with an assistant later in this chapter.

The most efficient and least frustrating solution for correcting your text is to have fewer mistakes to begin with. If your accuracy is around 95% or better, most of NaturallySpeaking's mistakes will be easy to correct without audio playback. You'll know what you said from the context of the surrounding words.

▶ The program types: "Sometimes a computer makes a mistake."
▶ It's easy to figure out what it should have typed: "Sometimes *the* computer makes a mistake."

To reduce errors, pronounce each word and speak clearly. The small amount of time taken by speaking more slowly and clearly will be paid back many times in less editing time and less frustration. Review the tips for better accuracy in Chapter 14 and implement as many as you can.

Step-by-Step: Correcting Your Dictation

If You Can Type

This correction method lets you work through the document smoothly, keeping your hands on the keyboard. Using the mouse, though easier to learn, is less efficient.

Work from top to bottom, proofreading what the computer typed. When you find a mistake:

▶ Select it:

    ▶ Move to the start of the mistake. (Pressing Ctrl+Left Arrow and Ctrl+Right Arrow let you jump word by word.)

    ▶ Hold down Ctrl+Shift and press Right Arrow once for each wrong word. This selects the whole mistake.

▶ If it's NaturallySpeaking's error:

    ▶ Press "-" on the keypad. The Correction window opens.

    ▶ Type the word or phrase you said and press Enter.

▶ If you misspoke or want to edit what you said, just type what you want. The new text replaces the selection.

▶ Keep proofreading, find the next error, and repeat.

Dictate a few paragraphs at a time, then go back and edit while what you said is still in mind. Or, if you're getting high recognition accuracy or lose your train of thought easily, dictate your whole document first before proofing.

If You Can't Type (or Don't Want To)

Correcting by voice can be frustrating when NaturallySpeaking misrecognizes your instructions. Follow these steps to stay on track.

Work from top to bottom, proofreading what the computer typed. For example, if you see the computer has typed "no way " instead of "away:"

▶ Select the mistake by saying "Select" plus the error ("Select no way").

    ▶ If the wrong words are selected, say the same phrase again ("Select no way").

    ▶ If the correct words are selected, but the wrong instance of them, say "Select Again."

    ▶ If NaturallySpeaking typed words instead of selecting text, it misrecognized your command. Say "Scratch That" and try again: "Select no way." If NaturallySpeaking still types instead of selects, you're probably not in a Select-and-Say application.

▶ Dictate the words you want. The new text replaces the selection.

▶ If the new text is wrong, correct it by saying "Spell That" plus the first few letters of the first word ("Spell That a-w-a"). The Correction window opens. Finish spelling the word or phrase you actually said and say "Choose 1."

▶ Keep proofreading, find the next error, and repeat.

Dictate a few paragraphs, then go back and edit while what you said is still fresh in your mind. Or, if you're getting high recognition accuracy or lose your train of thought easily, dictate your whole document first before proofing.

Don't Go Changing

Has this happened to you?

▶ You select NaturallySpeaking's mistake, then dictate the correct word. The program gets it wrong. You say "Scratch That" to delete the mistake. You dictate the correct word again.

▶ The program still gets it wrong. You say "Scratch That" to delete the mistake, frustrated at the computer's stupidity.

▶ You say the word again, this time more loudly and with more frustration. This time NaturallySpeaking gets it right.

In this example, you're changing your speaking style to make the computer type the word you want. By repeating the same word in different ways, you're not training the computer—it's training you! Worse, it's training you to be frustrated and frazzled and to speak in an unusual way.

Break this vicious pattern—use the Correction window. If you dictate a correction and the computer still gets it wrong, say "Correct That." This teaches the computer to recognize how you speak. You should not have to change how you speak to get good results.

Is This Computer Stupid or Something?!

Anger and frustration at the computer's repeated errors mimics our frustration when talking with a real person who doesn't understand. Talking with a human when communication isn't clear (over a poor phone line, say, or to someone hard of hearing) reflexively makes us try again—more slowly and loudly—if he doesn't understand. If he doesn't understand by the third time, frustration kicks in. Is he paying attention? Is he even listening? The anger in our tone encourages the listener to pay more attention to us.

Speaking to NaturallySpeaking, it's natural to do the same thing—speak more slowly and loudly to try and make the program understand. But NaturallySpeaking is not a person. It doesn't try any harder to understand you when you have a frustrated tone.

The computer's mistakes are part of using speech recognition, and the frustration they provoke is a natural human response. Keeping calm, though, makes NaturallySpeaking work better in the long run and makes using the program much more pleasant.

Proofing with a Recorder

Recording your dictation on a tape recorder (or digital recorder) provides a highly reliable way to proofread your dictation. If NaturallySpeaking will not play back segments of audio that you dictated, a tape may be the only way to remind yourself of what you originally said.

Listening to your recorded speech from tape is reliable but slow. Some recorders have a "fast playback" feature, which saves time in proofing. If you'll frequently use a recorder for proofing, choose one that has a foot pedal, which lets you keep your hands on the keyboard while starting and stopping the tape.

When proofing from a recorder, stop the tape while correcting a mistake, then move on. The amount of time required to proof your document depends, of course, on the number of errors as well as your typing speed. The key to efficiency here is to keep your hands on the keyboard and use keystrokes, not the mouse, to correct (see "Step-by-Step: Correcting Your Dictation" above). You can also make corrections by voice—listen to the tape, say "Select" plus the incorrect words, then dictate the correct text.

Working with an Assistant

Using speech recognition requires that someone correct the computer's mistakes. If you have an assistant, you can delegate corrections to him or her. This frees you to just dictate. NaturallySpeaking will create a draft, which the assistant will then proofread and edit.

An assistant will not be able to make all corrections accurately by proofreading NaturallySpeaking's written output. It's seldom obvious from reading how NaturallySpeaking's mistakes should be corrected. Also, if the computer skips a word or two in the transcription, the meaning of the text could be changed in a way that's undetectable by proofreading. ("The tumor was not benign" could be typed by NaturallySpeaking as "The tumor was benign.") The assistant must listen to the original tape to fix all NaturallySpeaking's mistakes accurately.

Perhaps you, like many professionals, now work by dictating into a recorder and paying someone to transcribe the tape. If instead you use NaturallySpeaking and delegate corrections, you can cut your transcription costs in half, or double your staff's output. NaturallySpeaking creates a draft of your dictation. An assistant listens to the taped dictation, correcting the draft along the way.

Traditional manual transcription takes three to four hours for each hour of dictation. With NaturallySpeaking, the computer creates a draft, using no staff time. Listening to a one-hour tape and editing the draft takes one and a half to two hours, depending on NaturallySpeaking's accuracy and the skill of the proofreader. Using speech recognition thus yields a 50 percent staff-time savings over traditional methods.

Delegated correction does have drawbacks. In many cases the proofreader is unable to teach the computer what you actually said, so NaturallySpeaking makes little or no improvement in accuracy. However, even if NaturallySpeaking makes the same mistakes repeatedly, it takes less time for the proofreader to correct the errors than it would for him or her to type the whole tape from scratch. The accuracy level may be lower than if you're making the corrections yourself, but the system is still highly cost effective.

Making delegated correction work well requires that the proofreader have training and practice in making fast corrections by keyboard. The proofreader also needs instruction in how to start NaturallySpeaking, choose the correct user, and have NaturallySpeaking transcribe the tape.

A successful delegated correction system also requires proper advance setup of the dictator's vocabulary files. When correction is delegated there's less opportunity for NaturallySpeaking to improve in accuracy and to learn new words. The dictator's NaturallySpeaking vocabulary should then match his or her dictation style as closely as possible right from the start. This requires using the Vocabulary Builder (see page 166). Physicians and attorneys should also use the appropriate base vocabulary.

(See Chapter 20 for information on obtaining medical and legal vocabularies.)

Workflow Outlines

This section details how people who delegate corrections can organize their work, and lists the equipment required.

Dictating into a Recorder

Dictating into a portable recorder and delegating corrections creates a workflow just like traditional transcription. All the dictator has to do is speak, then pass the tape to a transcriptionist. But instead of typing the whole tape by hand, the transcriptionist (now a proofreader) plays the tape into NaturallySpeaking to get a draft. He or she then listens to the original tape (with a foot pedal to control playback) and makes corrections as needed.

Recorded Dictation Outline

For the dictator:

1. Dictate into a recorder. Speak clearly.
2. Give the tape of your speech to an assistant, the proofreader.

For the proofreader:

1. Start NaturallySpeaking. Choose the correct user (the person who dictated the tape).
2. From the Tools menu, choose Transcribe (see page 207) and begin playing the tape into the computer.
3. When the tape is completed, save the draft transcription that NaturallySpeaking generated.
4. Listen to the tape, check NaturallySpeaking's transcript, and correct any errors. (See the above section, "Proofing with a Recorder," for tips.)

Once proofread and corrected, the document can be formatted, printed, or saved like any word processing document.

Equipment Needed

- ▶ computer with NaturallySpeaking (to transcribe)
- ▶ hand-held recorder compatible with NaturallySpeaking, for the dictator
- ▶ tape player with foot control for the proofreader (fast playback a plus)
- ▶ computer for proofreader to edit on (this can be the same system NaturallySpeaking is installed on; however, one cannot edit the text and have NaturallySpeaking transcribing at the same time.)

Dictating at the Computer

Alternately, you can dictate into the microphone while at the computer and still delegate corrections. Direct dictation has these advantages:

- ▶ Higher accuracy. Dictating directly into NaturallySpeaking with the headset microphone is always more accurate than recording the sound and playing it back.
- ▶ You can see what you just said as the computer types it.
- ▶ You'll have less tendency to mumble when speaking to the computer than you will when speaking into a recorder. Seeing correct and incorrect transcription by Naturally-Speaking reminds you to speak clearly and pronounce each word distinctly.
- ▶ No special tape recorder is needed—you can use the dictation equipment you already have.
- ▶ You can easily use macros to automate repetitive dictation.

Direct dictation has these disadvantages:

- ▶ You must be at the computer while dictating.
- ▶ There is no opportunity for the proofreader to use the Correction window to teach the computer and have it improve.

Direct Dictation Outline

For the dictator:

1. Dictate your writing into NaturallySpeaking through the computer's microphone. Have a tape recorder running to record your dictation.
2. On a floppy disk, save the draft transcription that NaturallySpeaking generates. Give the disk to your assistant. (If you have an office network, you can save the draft directly onto the network for access by the assistant.)
3. Give the tape of your dictation to your assistant.

For the proofreader:

1. Start your word processor and open the draft transcription (the text that NaturallySpeaking created).
2. Listen to the tape, check NaturallySpeaking's transcript, and correct any errors. (See the above section, "Proofing with a Recorder," for tips.)

Once proofread and corrected, the document can be formatted, printed, or saved like any other word processing document.

Equipment Needed

▶ computer with NaturallySpeaking, for the dictator (to transcribe)
▶ tape recorder near the dictator's computer, to record as he or she speaks to NaturallySpeaking
▶ tape player with foot control for the proofreader (fast playback a plus)
▶ editing computer for the proofreader

The direct dictation and recorder methods are not exclusive—one can dictate into the computer sometimes and use a portable recorder at other times.

Many Dictators with One Proofreader

For offices where several people dictate, extend the delegated correction methods described above. For offices using portable recorders, a recorder for each dictator is required.

Equipment Needed Using Recorders

▶ computer with NaturallySpeaking (to transcribe)
▶ each dictator needs a hand-held recorder compatible with NaturallySpeaking
▶ tape player with foot control for proofreader (fast playback a plus)
▶ computer for proofreader to edit on (this can be the same system NaturallySpeaking is installed on; however, the proofreader cannot edit the text at the same time Naturally-Speaking is transcribing.)

If transcription volume is heavy, the NaturallySpeaking computer will definitely need to be separate from the editing computer so that the proofreader can listen to one tape while NaturallySpeaking transcribes another.

For offices using direct dictation (as opposed to using recorders), each dictator also needs his or her own computer.

Equipment Needed with Direct Dictation

▶ computer with NaturallySpeaking for each dictator
▶ tape recorder near each dictator's computer, to record as he or she speaks to NaturallySpeaking
▶ tape player with foot control for proofreader (fast playback a plus)
▶ editing computer for proofreader

Transcribing Interviews by "Shadowing"

People often ask if NaturallySpeaking can transcribe taped interviews and lectures. The software cannot transcribe these tapes directly because conversational speech has neither the clarity nor the punctuation that NaturallySpeaking requires. Also, NaturallySpeaking needs to be previously trained on the voice of the person speaking, which is seldom the case in an interview.

Though NaturallySpeaking cannot transcribe tapes directly, you can still use the software to make transcribing quicker and less tedious than typing. To do this, listen to the recording and pause the tape after each passage or sentence. Then repeat the words you heard, dictating them to the computer. Include punctuation and speak clearly as you translate the recording to speech NaturallySpeaking can recognize. Depending on your goals, you may not have to transcribe the whole tape verbatim. Reviewing a taped interview, for example, you might dictate only key facts or notable quotations.

This verbal "shadowing" can be a great time-saver. With practice, some people can dictate to the computer simultaneously to listening to the tape, as a United Nations translator might speak in French while listening to a speech in English.

The Mechanical Voice

NaturallySpeaking can read your text to you in a synthesized voice, which some people find helpful for proofreading. This feature, available only in Word, WordPerfect, and the Naturally-Speaking window, is called "text-to-speech."

To use text-to-speech, select the text you want Naturally-Speaking to read. Then do one of these:

▶ Say "Read That."
▶ Choose Read That from the NaturallySpeaking Tools menu.
▶ In NaturallySpeaking, press Ctrl+Alt+S.

These commands also read text:

▶ "Read Line"
▶ "Read Paragraph"
▶ "Read Document"
▶ "Read Window" (only the words in view)
▶ "Read to Here" (read from the top of the window to the cursor)
▶ "Read from Here" (read from the cursor to the bottom of the window)

To stop NaturallySpeaking as it reads, press the Esc key or click the Stop Playback button on the NaturallySpeaking toolbar. You cannot stop playback by voice. To change the sound of the synthesized voice, use the Options dialog box (see page 214).

13

Speaking and Dictating

When you're trying to impress someone at a cocktail party, you'll probably try to speak in complete, grammatical sentences. If you lose your train of thought in the middle of a phrase, your new acquaintance might look at you strangely.

Talking to the computer is a different matter. The computer doesn't care about your grammar or word choice, or even if you stop speaking for minutes at a time.

Most of us have had limited experience conversing with our little gray boxes—besides cursing at them when they crash. To speak effectively with NaturallySpeaking, you'll need to unlearn old habits and gain new skills.

How to Speak to NaturallySpeaking

Speak Clearly

In conversation, people tend to mumble and slur words together, knowing others will still understand what they say. If you say "Jeet?" your friend will understand it as "Did you eat?" Computers, however, are less adaptable than people. To achieve accurate results from NaturallySpeaking you must speak clearly. Pretend you're Dan Rather or Katie Couric reading the news, or imagine that you're giving a presentation to a small group. You may end up speaking more loudly than usual, and that's fine. For a useful exercise, see "Moving Your Mouth," below.

Moving Your Mouth

Read out loud a sentence from this book. Make a point of slurring your words and mumbling. Then read the sentence again, clearly. Can you tell what you're doing differently in these two readings?

Make a big smile. Notice what it feels like to raise the corners of your mouth. Next, pucker up your lips and push them out, as if you're making an exaggerated kiss. Notice the muscles around your mouth that make your lips move. Then, drag the corners of your mouth into a frown.

Try reading the same sentence three more times—once smiling, once puckered-up, and once frowning.

Did you notice a difference in sound quality? Pitch? Clarity?

Now let your jaw relax. Gently massage your jaw muscles, your temples, the sides and front of your chin, the muscles beneath your eyes, and the area above your upper lip.

Finally, sit up straight at your computer and read the same sentence again. The idea is not to speak more loudly, or to "push" words out. Just read calmly and clearly. How does this feel different from mumbling?

Voice exercises like those singers use can also be useful. It may help to imagine that talking is giving the corners of your mouth a workout. Don't exaggerate your sounds or force them. Speak normally, just more clearly.

Pronounce Each Word

When we listen to someone speak, our ears receive an unbroken stream of sound. Our brains automatically separate this sound into words. We reconstruct words that are only partially heard—or left out altogether. Here's an example.

Read this sentence out loud to a friend, standing so that she cannot see your face. Notice that the sentence is missing a word—to be grammatical, it should say "to *a* computer."

"The book I'm reading is about speaking to computer."

Have your friend repeat back what she heard. Chances are she'll fill in the "a" to make the sentence grammatical.

Because our brains reconstruct missing sounds so easily (especially small, common words like "a," "the," and "of"), in everyday speech we tend not to pronounce every sound and word. It's just not necessary.

A computer transcribing speech tries to reconstruct missing sounds, too, taking its best guess at what you actually said. However, it often guesses incorrectly. For accurate transcription, it's important to make sure every word you say to the computer is pronounced, not "missing." A sentence that is perfectly understandable to a person might not be clear enough to a computer.

This change in speaking style does not mean that you have to slow your natural pace. It's fine to dictate to NaturallySpeaking as rapidly as you like. Just be sure to speak clearly and pronounce each word.

Pause If You Like

Your friends might think it odd if during an animated conversation you halt mid-sentence to gather your thoughts. When speaking to the computer, though, you can pause as long as you like, to think, take a break, or arrange your notes. NaturallySpeaking won't get bored waiting for you.

Give It Context

Your accuracy will increase if you speak in complete sentences because the computer has more context to use in deciphering your sounds. Speaking one word at a time usually decreases accuracy. So concentrate, think of the right words, and speak them as a continuous stream.

Leave Out the Fillers

NaturallySpeaking will usually mistake "uh" and "um" for "a," "of," and similar-sounding words. Unfortunately, since "uh" and "um" sound so much like these words, there is no way to make NaturallySpeaking ignore them. To learn to stop saying "um," practice being silent instead of saying something to fill the space. When you feel an "um" coming on, just say nothing. Saying "um" can be as addictive as nail biting. But if you can excise these filler words from your speech, you'll also sound more articulate and confident.

Speak with Inflection

When talking to the computer, people tend to imitate the robotic voices of computers in old sci-fi movies. But using a flat monotone will reduce your accuracy as well as put you to sleep. Keep photos of friends next to the computer and pretend you're speaking to them. This will help you use more natural tones and will brighten your day, too.

Breathe

Breathing fully and sitting straight will help you speak clearly. If you slouch while dictating, your lungs will be compressed and your voice constrained, making it harder for the computer to understand your words. See Chapter 15 for more information on good posture at the computer. The breathing exercise below can help you notice what it's like to breathe more fully.

Breathing

While seated, put your hand lightly on your belly. Breathe in and out slowly from the top of your chest, without letting your hand move. This is breathing "shallowly." Now breathe in so that your belly expands, moving the hand that's resting on it. When you breathe out, your belly (and hand upon it) should move back to its original place. This deeper breathing can help you speak more clearly and may make you feel healthier in general.

Close Your Eyes

Dictating while looking at the screen tends to be distracting—it makes your speech more hesitant and less natural. Try dictating with your eyes closed. Most people get significantly better results this way. If your boss thinks you're taking a nap, try looking at the wall or at the photos of your friends.

Be Alert

When it's 4:00 a.m. and you're still dictating the proposal that's due tomorrow, your recognition results will suffer as much as you're suffering. Tired people tend to mumble and speak without energy. You'll get your best results when you're most alert.

Relax

Stress and tension change voice quality and degrade recognition accuracy. When you're new to speech recognition software, you might be a bit anxious as you speak, anticipating that the computer will make mistakes. The computer does, of course, and frustration may kick in as you see the mistakes proliferate. Frustration makes you more tense, changing your voice, which generates more mistakes, more frustration, and still more mistakes.

Errors are inherent in computer transcription (as in human transcription). The computer takes its best guess at what you say, and it often guesses incorrectly. Correcting mistakes is part of the normal process of using speech recognition. When you learned to type, correcting errors became second nature. With the right attitude, correcting recognition errors can become just as routine.

It helps to have a sense of humor about the computer's errors, and the computer is great at generating real howlers of mistakes. Speech recognition software tries to fit what you say into something that makes grammatical sense, if not literal sense. So its weird guesses often fit right into your sentence. You say "fresh squeezed lemonade" and the computer types it out: "fresh grease lemon aid." Don't try *that* beverage at home. (See Chapter 19 for more blooper examples.)

Working at the computer is not especially good for your body. Humans were not made to sit in place for hours at a time, arms forward, fingers twitching rapidly. The repetitive motions of typing can cause discomfort and, in some cases, serious injury. (For tips on healthy computing, see Chapter 15.) It doesn't help that the intensity of computer work can lead people to neglect their bodies, posture, and physical positioning for hours at a time. Many computer users make an association, conscious or unconscious, between using the computer and being tense.

Muscle tension can make your voice tense, changing its pitch and quality. Because NaturallySpeaking tends not to respond as well to tense voices, achieving high accuracy takes some unlearning of the "computers = tension" equation.

Working towards better results with speech recognition software can actually help you develop healthy habits. Good posture, rest, exercise, and meditation not only improve general well-being but also, amazingly, make NaturallySpeaking recognize your voice better. At last, computer use that encourages good health!

Learning to Dictate

Like any other skill, dictating to NaturallySpeaking takes practice to do well. I wrote my high school papers by hand, before the personal computer age, and in college, after computers had become widespread, I continued to write papers longhand, typing them into the computer from my notes. Gradually I became more adept at typing and started composing by typing into a computer directly.

Years later, a repetitive strain injury caused by too much computer use forced me to give up keyboards. With much writing to do and unable to afford a secretary, I turned to speech recognition software as a keyboard replacement. At first, composing out loud—never mind speaking to the computer—felt strange and unnatural. The mechanics of watching the computer screen, correcting mistakes, and editing text by voice constantly interrupted my thought process. I dealt with this by handwriting first, then dictating the handwritten words into my computer.

Writing by voice engages a different thought process than typing or writing longhand. Like the transition from handwriting to typing, it took effort and practice for me to master this change. But after years of practice, I now write most everything by voice—including this book! For myself and for hundreds of thousands of other speech software users, dictation now comes naturally—as much or more so than the unnatural, but learned, skills of typing and handwriting.

Composing

Start by Reading

We all learned to type by copying printed passages. The best way to learn to dictate is to begin the same way—by copying. By dictating something already on paper, you can practice learning the voice software without having to worry about composing sentences at the same time.

Choose a letter, memo, or e-mail message typical of the type of writing you do. Then read it into the computer as if you're speaking to another person. Say "comma" and "period" as needed, and for a new paragraph say "new paragraph." (See Chapter 8 for more punctuation and for other commands to say while dictating.) Look away from the computer, focusing on the page. As you read, pretend the computer isn't even there.

Reading aloud will help you get used to talking to the computer. After a bit of practice, add in a few sentences of your own thoughts. By starting to compose out loud interspersed with reading, you'll overcome any natural inhibitions you might have.

Fear of Dictating

If you feel inhibited or self-critical when talking to the computer, remember that the computer doesn't care what you say or how you say it. It's easiest to start writing by voice when no one is around, and you should ensure this privacy when learning. Practice will make you less self-conscious. If NaturallySpeaking makes mistakes while you're practicing, just laugh at them and fix them later.

Easy and Chatty

When learning to compose by voice, start with what's easy. Try dictating a few sentences about today's weather, make a list of things to do, or compose a chatty letter to a friend.

It's easier to dictate when you're not looking at the screen. Look at the ceiling or close your eyes. This will help you avoid distraction, relax, and let the thoughts flow.

Complex Writing

Save more difficult documents for later, after you're comfortable composing simpler texts by voice. In the meantime, continue to prepare complex writing your usual way, such as by typing. To dictate on complex topics, you'll need the skills of both speaking properly to the computer and composing intricate prose by dictation. It's best to practice these skills one at a time.

Only after you're skilled at more casual, "chatty" compositions should you dictate documents that:

- ▶ have difficult or complex subject matter
- ▶ follow a detailed outline
- ▶ use complex sentence structure
- ▶ are aimed at a demanding audience, such as professional colleagues
- ▶ will be widely circulated

Dictation Tips

- ▶ Speak in complete sentences, or at least complete phrases. Think of what you're going to say before you say it. Composing a sentence in your head before saying it will help you maintain your train of thought.
- ▶ For complex writing, outlining is key. For a detailed letter, write or dictate a few words summarizing the main point and subpoints of each paragraph. When you're dictating, look at the outline. You'll naturally expand the outline to complete sentences as you speak.
- ▶ When you're writing a first draft, capture your ideas as quickly as you can get them on the screen. Don't try to edit as you go—you can come back and edit later. Tell yourself to keep talking.
- ▶ If you need extra motivation to get over dictation hesitancy, think of all you have to gain from writing out loud. Imagine boosting your output by double. Imagine filling the screen with text without having to type. Relax your hands, arms, and shoulders, and think how nice it is not to have to bang away at the keyboard.
- ▶ As in any writing, keep your audience in mind. Imagine the particular person you're writing for to help the dictation flow.

▶ Composing aloud, your writing style may change. Some people find that their spoken style is less polished and more conversational. It may be easy and rapid for you to dictate first drafts, then go back and revise later. You might be pleased with your new spoken style, teach yourself how to compose aloud in your "old" style, or use a combination of dictating and revising to get the results you want. Use whatever method you prefer.

▶ Using speech recognition can be a good way to get over writer's block. Imagine you're telling a friend what's next, then tell the computer.

Henry James Dictated Too

Author Henry James wrote his novels longhand—until 1896. Pain in his right wrist, probably from writer's cramp, led him to hire a stenographer so that he could write out loud. The switch to dictation changed his style. Wrote a biographer, "the spoken voice was to be heard henceforth in James's prose, not only in the rhythm and ultimate perfection of his verbal music, but in his use of colloquialisms, and in a greater indulgence in metaphor." Friends claimed they could pinpoint the exact chapter in *What Maisie Knew* when handwriting ended and dictation began. (From *Henry James: A Life,* by Leon Edel)

Plan: Learning to Dictate

1. Read to the computer to get used to talking to it. Review the tips on how to speak to NaturallySpeaking to get the best possible accuracy while reading.

2. Compose simple sentences about the weather, then move on to notes to friends.

3. Outline a letter or memo several paragraphs long. Dictate the letter from start to finish based on the outline.

4. Continue outlining and dictating. If you like, experiment with making a mental outline instead of a written one. Some users eventually compose entirely

in their heads, while others continue to make outlines even if they write only a word or two for each outline point.

Improving Performance

Imagine a NaturallySpeaking that performs perfectly—making no mistakes and typing your words instantaneously. A Utopian vision? Maybe. But you can take concrete steps toward improving your accuracy, the most important factor in using the program productively.

A 90 percent accuracy rate means about 25 mistakes per page, while a 95 percent accuracy rate is around 13 mistakes per page. The five percent difference in accuracy means half the time spent correcting and a much lower level of frustration. A small improvement in accuracy can be the difference between speech software being a productive, useful tool versus being too frustrating to use.

For the easiest and fastest way to improve accuracy, see "One Minute to Fewer Errors," page 158.

What level of accuracy you can expect depends on many variables, including the speed of your computer, your sound hardware, the type of text you dictate, and how clearly you speak. After you complete NaturallySpeaking's initial training, the program should type at least 80 percent of your dictation accurately. As you use the program over several weeks, correcting mistakes in the Correction window, the software will learn your voice, and its accuracy improves. Most people can achieve an accuracy rate of between 92 and 98 percent.

To check your accuracy, read to NaturallySpeaking from some written text for two or three minutes. Count the number of mistakes NaturallySpeaking made and divide by the total number of words you said. If, for example, NaturallySpeaking made 16 mistakes in 200 words, your error rate is eight percent (16 divided by 200). Your accuracy rate is 92 percent (184 correct words divided by 200). The error rate plus the accuracy rate totals 100 percent.

Low Accuracy

If you're getting less than 80 percent accuracy (more than two mistakes per sentence, on average), you probably need to change your microphone or sound card, or make other adjustments to your computer. See the troubleshooting suggestions for low accuracy, page 256.

The Speech Recognition Ideal

Like a problem-free romance, the most accurate possible system is an unattainable ideal. You'd have to:

- ▶ always speak clearly and articulate each word
- ▶ sound exactly the same at all times and on all days
- ▶ have trained NaturallySpeaking to recognize your voice exactly as it is at any given moment
- ▶ keep the microphone exactly the same distance from your mouth, in the same position
- ▶ use an ultra-high-fidelity microphone that transmits sounds exactly as you say them
- ▶ use a sound card that faithfully converts the microphone signal to digital form
- ▶ speak only words NaturallySpeaking has heard before

- ▶ compose only sentences similar to ones NaturallySpeaking has heard before
- ▶ have the fastest available processor in your computer
- ▶ have at least 128 MB of RAM
- ▶ have a hard drive with enough free space
- ▶ work in a quiet room
- ▶ have no radio interference or electrical noise from power lines
- ▶ use the latest version of NaturallySpeaking
- ▶ run only NaturallySpeaking and no other programs

Many of these items are impossible. No one's voice, for example, always sounds the same, and no microphone reproduces sounds 100 percent accurately. Other items are impractical. What fun is using NaturallySpeaking only in its own word processing window? It's more useful to dictate right into Word, Netscape, or your e-mail program. And only people who have a top-of-the line computer that's less than two weeks old have the fastest available processor. Here's a guide to improvements that are practical.

Speak Clearly

Speaking clearly and articulating each word is essential to getting high accuracy. The truism "garbage in, garbage out" applies here. The clearer your speech, the better NaturallySpeaking will guess what you said. If you mumble and slur your words, you'll get errors all over, even if your computer is more powerful than NASA's. (See Chapter 13 for tips on how to speak.)

Retrain

People's voices change on different days and even within the same day. NaturallySpeaking matches your sounds to a computer model of your voice. The more different your voice is from the model, the more mistakes the program will make. You can't make your voice sound the same all the time, but you can make NaturallySpeaking retune its voice model to the way your voice sounds right now. See "One Minute to Fewer Errors," below.

One Minute to Fewer Errors

People's speech sounds different on different days and at different times. My voice, for example, sounds more gravelly in the morning than in the afternoon, and more nasal in the summer than in the winter. NaturallySpeaking, though, gives the best results if your voice always sounds the same. To make NaturallySpeaking work better, retrain the program for a minute or two so it recognizes how your voice sounds right then. This is the easiest and fastest way to improve accuracy.

To retrain, from the NaturallySpeaking Tools menu choose General Training. Select a text to read from the options shown. Then click Record and read the on-screen passages. This process is just like when you first read to NaturallySpeaking for half an hour to teach it your voice. In this case, though, you do not need to spend so long reading. Just read until the Recorded Speech timer shows at least a minute has elapsed. Click Finish and NaturallySpeaking will save your voice files, newly adjusted to how your voice is right now. You should experience better accuracy right away. Do this whenever NaturallySpeaking is making more errors than usual—as frequently as twice a day if it helps.

Keep the Microphone in the Same Position

Each time you use NaturallySpeaking, keep the microphone the same distance from your mouth. Review microphone placement, page 13.

If NaturallySpeaking adds unwanted short words to your dictation (like "a," "in," and "of"), the microphone may be picking up your breathing. Move the microphone closer to the corner of your mouth. If the mic is already at the corner of your mouth, move it about an inch farther away from your face. Also, check that the microphone cord is not rustling against your clothes.

Use a Good Microphone

All microphones distort the sound of your voice as it's transmitted to the computer, but some microphones work much better than others. The microphone included in most NaturallySpeaking packages costs just a few dollars to manufacture and has limited fidelity. Most people get significantly better accuracy by switching to a higher-quality microphone. The Parrott-10 microphone, manufactured by VXI, sells for about $90 and is one of several good choices for a mic upgrade. The Parrott-10 is included with NaturallySpeaking Professional, Medical, and Legal editions. Other microphone manufacturers include Andrea Electronics, Philips, and Shure. (For manufacturer contact information, see Chapter 20.)

Headset microphones tend to give better accuracy than handheld microphones, which tend to move around more relative to your mouth. This makes your voice sound less consistent to NaturallySpeaking.

Use a Good Sound Card

Your system's sound card is as important as your microphone in conveying a clear sound signal to NaturallySpeaking. Upgrading to a high-quality microphone will show no accuracy improvement if your sound card generates static or an insufficient signal level.

You can test your sound system using the NaturallySpeaking Audio Setup Wizard, in both automatic and advanced modes. You can also test by ear, listening to your recorded speech through your computer's speakers. (See "Testing Your Sound System" on page 240 for detailed instructions.)

Sound System Recommendations

Follow these steps to improve your microphone and sound card combination.

1. Try what you have—the sound card included with your computer and the microphone included with NaturallySpeaking. Use NaturallySpeaking for at least a week, correcting errors in the Correction window and speaking clearly.

2. If you're not satisfied with your accuracy, use the sound recorder to listen to how your voice sounds to NaturallySpeaking (see "Testing By Ear," page 243). If the recorded voice sounds clear and free of static, the sound card and microphone are working fine. Otherwise, continue to step 3.

3. If you have an integrated sound card, install a new sound card and retrain NaturallySpeaking for at least ten minutes (follow the instructions in "One Minute to Fewer Errors," page 158).

4. If you're using a low-cost microphone (like the one included with NaturallySpeaking Standard and Preferred editions, or a microphone included with your computer or sound card), buy a better microphone.

Context

NaturallySpeaking guesses what words you said from context as well as from the sound of your voice. If the words you say are similar to what you've said before, the program tends to guess what you say more accurately. Use the Vocabulary Builder (see page 166) to teach NaturallySpeaking your writing style and what words you tend to use most often. This will significantly improve its accuracy.

Processor Speed, Memory, and Disk Space

Processor power boosts recognition performance, though it's less important than context and a clear speech signal. A faster processor, or CPU, in your computer lets the software make more calculations in the same amount of time, so it can better hone in on what words you actually said. For optimal results, the speech software should not have to share processor power with any other programs running at the same time.

Your computer should have enough memory (RAM) to hold NaturallySpeaking and any other programs running at the same time. If you are using NaturallySpeaking with no other programs open, 64 MB of RAM should be sufficient. If you use Naturally-Speaking with Word or other programs, as most people do, upgrading to 128 MB of RAM may improve recognition accuracy by allowing NaturallySpeaking to load more powerful recognition methods into memory. Upgrading will also decrease your frustration by reducing some of the program's delays when you correct.

Hard disk space is relatively unimportant to program performance, as long as you have about 500 MB free for the Windows operating system to use for temporary storage as you work. If your hard disk is more than about five percent fragmented, defragmenting your drive may improve Naturally-Speaking's performance slightly. You can check your disk by choosing Programs from the Windows Start menu, then choosing Accessories, System Tools, Disk Defragmenter.

Improving Speed

On all systems, there's a delay between when you speak and when NaturallySpeaking types out what you said. Naturally-Speaking uses this delay time, plus the time when you're talking, to recognize your speech. The faster your processor, the shorter the delay. Using a CPU that's 400 MHz or faster reduces the delay to almost nothing, and your speech appears about as rapidly as you talk. Even with a speedy processor, though, NaturallySpeaking usually waits until you pause to type out what it recognized.

Sound quality is at least as important as CPU speed in making NaturallySpeaking work quickly. If your microphone and sound card combination make your speech sound fuzzy to the computer or if they generate background hiss or static, Naturally-Speaking will have to spend much more time processing your speech to eliminate the background noise. A clear microphone and sound card combination will substantially boost speed as well as accuracy.

If your computer has 64 MB of RAM or less, or if you have many programs open besides NaturallySpeaking, you may experience delays of two to three seconds or more when dictating your first sentence after starting NaturallySpeaking and when using the Correction window. These delays diminish or disappear when more memory is available. Run fewer programs while running NaturallySpeaking, add more memory to your computer, or do both.

Background Noise

NaturallySpeaking performs best in a quiet room. In a noisy office, accuracy will decrease slightly, though the program will still be useful. For best results, train (or retrain) your voice files in the same environment as you'll be dictating.

If a consistent, loud noise like an air conditioner or fan interferes with good recognition, consider a microphone with active noise cancellation. This type of mic removes background noise from the sound of your voice, delivering a clear speech signal to the computer. (See Chapter 20 for manufacturer contact information.)

Electrical Interference

In some cases, noise in a building's electrical wiring will generate static in your computer's sound card. Few desktop users encounter this problem; it's mostly limited to laptops, which have less isolation of power source and sound card. If your laptop is performing slowly or inaccurately, try unplugging it and operating from battery power only to eliminate possible interference from the building wiring.

NaturallySpeaking with Other Software

If you have NaturallySpeaking version 3.x or below, upgrade to version 4 for significant accuracy improvements. ("Naturally-Speaking 3.x" means any version of NaturallySpeaking that begins with 3, such as 3.0 or 3.52.) To find out what version you have, choose About NaturallySpeaking from the NaturallySpeaking Help menu.

When dictating into the NaturallySpeaking window with no other programs running, your computer's power is dedicated to processing your speech. If other programs are also open, or if you're dictating into another program, your computer must divide its processing power between processing your speech and other tasks. Some programs use more computing resources than others. WordPad and Eudora, for example, take little processing power, so dictating into these programs or using NaturallySpeaking while these programs are open will not decrease Naturally-Speaking's accuracy or speed significantly.

Microsoft Word, however, uses a great deal of system resources, and dictating into Word is usually slower and less accurate than dictating into NaturallySpeaking directly. How much worse NaturallySpeaking performs depends on how much speed and memory you have. On a Pentium 400 machine with 128 MB of RAM, there is little performance difference. On a Pentium 200 machine with 64 MB of RAM, the difference in performance is substantial. Other programs vary in the resources they use. Your NaturallySpeaking performance will vary depending on how many other programs are open, what programs they are, and the speed and memory in your computer.

Some programs that use system resources run in the background, without appearing in an on-screen window. Virus software and "reminder" alarm clock programs are among the programs in this category. To find and remove software running in the background, see "Software Conflicts" on page 250.

Better Accuracy with a Recorder

Transcribing from a recorder tends to be less accurate than dictating directly into the computer for several reasons.

- The built-in microphone in the recorder may be lower quality than the headset microphone you use for dictation directly to the computer.
- Like using a handheld microphone, using a handheld recorder keeps the microphone in a less consistent place from your mouth than does a headset microphone.
- Minicassette recorders and other analog models lose sound information in both recording and playback. They record only part of your voice, then play back only part of what they record to be processed by the sound card. Digital recorders that digitally transfer sound do not have this limitation. They also record only part of your voice, but they bypass the sound card, sending the digital recording file directly to NaturallySpeaking for transcription.
- Using a recorder, people more often mumble and slur their words. They forget they are talking for a computer to transcribe.

To get the best accuracy from a recorder, use an external microphone if your recorder has a questionable built-in microphone. Nearly all recorders allow you to plug in an external mic to replace the unit's built-in one. A headset microphone is best, since it keeps the mic at a constant distance from your mouth. Try using the headset mic included with your speech software.

Most people don't want to carry around a headset microphone with their recorder, even if it will give them better accuracy. "Stalk" microphones are also available. These stick out a inch or two from the recorder like a small mushroom.

If you're using the recorder's built-in mic, keep it a consistent distance from your mouth. It should be at the corner of your mouth, about an inch away. See the instructions included with your recorder, or experiment to find the best distance.

Using a digital recorder might or might not improve your accuracy. It depends on the recorder and whether you use an external microphone. The Norcom 2500, for example, an analog minicassette unit, gives about the same accuracy as the digital Dragon Voice-It recorder when you use the built-in microphone in each. The Voice-It model has excellent sound reproduction but an average built-in microphone. The Norcom unit has an excellent built-in mic but degrades the speech signal a bit in recording and in playback through the sound card.

One solution is to use a good headset microphone with the Dragon Voice-It model—this combination gives excellent recognition results. However, this requires that you carry around the headset with the recorder. Better accuracy often comes at the cost of convenience.

Speaking clearly will improve transcription accuracy no matter what recorder you have. Remember that you're talking for a computer, not a person. Speak clearly, speak with energy, and pronounce each word.

Backing Up Speech Files

It's important to back up your speech files regularly. As you use NaturallySpeaking, it adapts to your voice and learns your personal added words. Making regular backups, perhaps every week, saves having to start from scratch should something happen to your computer.

NaturallySpeaking will make a backup automatically every fifth time you save your speech files. (You can change this frequency in the Options dialog box, see page 217.) The program will also save a copy of your files when you choose Backup from the User menu. NaturallySpeaking's backups are stored on the same computer as your original files, though. To backup more reliably, copy your voice files to a backup tape or Zip drive and store them away from your computer.

To back up your voice files, start Windows Explorer and find the NatSpeak folder. For most users, this folder is in the C: directory (the root directory of the C: drive). Open the NatSpeak folder. Inside will be a folder called Users, and inside that is a separate folder for each user on the machine. Open the folder with your name. Inside your User folder is a folder called Current. This folder is the one to back up. To summarize, here is what a typical path looks like:

C:\NatSpeak\Users\Dan\current

This folder, more than 40 MB in size, is too large to fit on a floppy disk. For a safe backup, copy this folder to a Zip disk or data tape. Store the disk or tape at another location (at home, for example, if your computer is at work).

If your computer is on an office network, you may be able to copy your speech files to the server or storage area on your network, where it can be safely backed up by your company's information systems staff.

A Suggested Backup System

There are two types of computer users: those who have lost data and those who haven't yet. We all know that backing up is important, but many of us avoid it because it's a hassle. Here is a backup system that's simple enough to use regularly.

Preparation

Keep all documents to be backed up in one folder, with subfolders. For example, keep your files in the My Documents folder, inside subfolders for business, personal, and other categories meaningful to you. Avoid storing files with the application that created them (Word files with the Word program, Excel files with Excel) because this makes backing up less convenient. Some applications, like e-mail programs, require that the files you create be stored with the application. However, for files you can choose where to place, place them all within the same folder.

Buy a Zip, Syquest, or recordable CD-ROM drive. Tape drives tend to be slow and cumbersome.

Use the backup software that came with your drive to select the folders and files to back up. Include the My Documents folder, your NaturallySpeaking voice files, and your e-mail and other files that couldn't be saved into the My Documents folder.

Set your backup program on Verify to have the computer double-check each backup for accuracy. Save these settings.

Prepare three sets of backup disks. Depending on how many files you have, you may need three or more disks in each set. Label the disks "set A disk 1," "set A disk 2," and so on.

Each Week

Run a backup using the settings you created in the backup software. If you're at work, store the backup disk set you just created safely at home, and return the old backup disks from home to work to reuse. Take the newest set somewhere apart from your computer (in this example, home, or to a safe deposit box) and bring the oldest set back home to be reused. The three disk sets you created should rotate. One set should always be at home, one at work, and the third in transit.

For More Security

For more protection against losing data, make an additional set of backup disks every three months and store them in a safe deposit box or with a friend. If something happens to your computer or to your weekly backups, you'll have these disks to fall back on.

To verify that your backup system is working, use the Retrieve or Restore function in your backup software to recover an old file from a backup set. Do this at least every three months.

Using the Vocabulary Builder

When NaturallySpeaking analyzes what you say, it uses a statistical model of what words tend to go together and what words you use most often. NaturallySpeaking's built-in model is designed for general business writing. It works best when you dictate business letters, memos, and other documents of similar language. If you dictate a laboratory report or a poem, Naturally-Speaking will tend to make relatively more errors.

For best accuracy, you need to show NaturallySpeaking samples of the types of documents you write and the words you use most often. To do this, use the Vocabulary Builder, a built-in tool that lets NaturallySpeaking learn your writing style. Using the Vocabulary Builder affects NaturallySpeaking's models of how often words are used, but it does not change Naturally-Speaking's model of how your voice sounds.

How the Vocabulary Builder Improves Accuracy

The Vocabulary Builder uses your processed documents three ways.

First, your writing changes the program's expectations about how often you say different words and phrases. If you're a teacher who often uses the word "grades," NaturallySpeaking will be much less likely after processing to mistakenly type "graves."

Second, the program finds words that are only in its backup vocabulary. These words will always be misrecognized, so Naturally-Speaking moves them to your active vocabulary. This way it can find them in RAM as it transcribes your speech. The program's backup vocabulary is over 200,000 words, so there are few words it does not already know. (For more about how active and backup vocabularies work, see page 47.)

The software also finds words it has never seen before in either the active or backup vocabulary. It lists these words for you and asks if you'd like to add any of them.

Prepare Documents for Processing

To best teach the computer, find documents typical of those you normally dictate. If you tend to write memos, letters, and reports, find a few representative samples of each. NaturallySpeaking will use these files as a guide to the type of writing it expects to hear. Aim for 50 to 100 pages of material, though more or less than that amount is fine too. Note the filename and location of each document. Documents can be saved in any of these file formats:

Format	File extension
Text	.txt
Rich text	.rtf
HTML	.htm, .html, .shtm, .shtml
Microsoft Word 6 or later	.doc
WordPerfect 8 or 9	.wpd

You must have Word installed to process Word files, and you must have WordPerfect installed to process WordPerfect files.

If you create more than one type of writing, such as business memos and novels, or medical reports and personal correspondence, you'll get best accuracy by creating a separate vocabulary for each type of writing. See "Multiple Vocabularies," page 174.

Process Documents

From the Tools menu in NaturallySpeaking, choose Vocabulary Builder. A welcome screen appears. Confirm that the user and vocabulary listed towards the bottom of this screen are the ones you want to work with, then click Next for the "Add Words From a List" screen (Figure 14-1). This screen is for the specialized task of adding a list of words and phrases, an advanced feature described on page 173. Click Next to skip to the screen "Analyze Documents," shown in Figure 14-2. Click the Add button (Figure 14-2) to choose documents to be processed.

Figure 14-1
Press Next to skip this screen, which is for an advanced Vocabulary Builder technique.

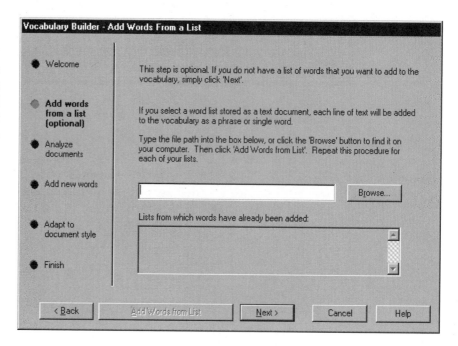

Figure 14-2
Click Add to begin
selecting documents
to process.

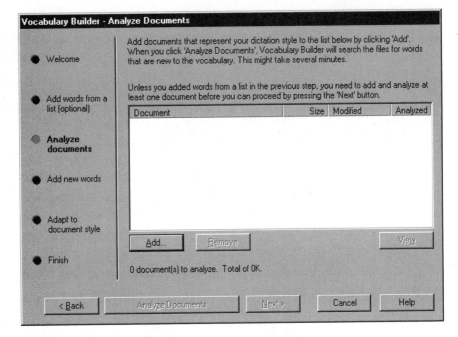

Click on a document to select it (Figure 14-3). You can select more than one document at once by holding down the Ctrl key and clicking the mouse on each one. You can select a range of documents by clicking once on the first document you're selecting, then holding down the Shift key and clicking once on the last document.

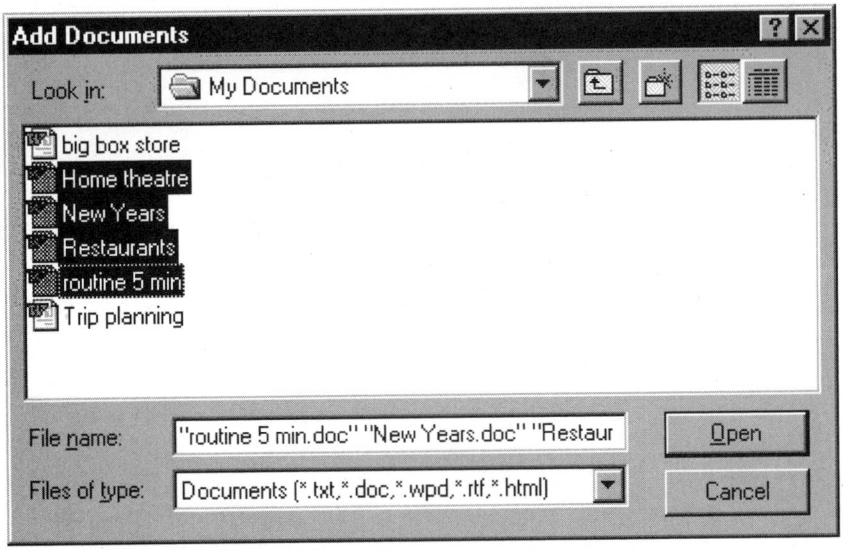

Figure 14-3
Select documents to
be processed and
click Open.

Figure 14-4
Click Add to add
more files, or
click Analyze
Documents to
continue.

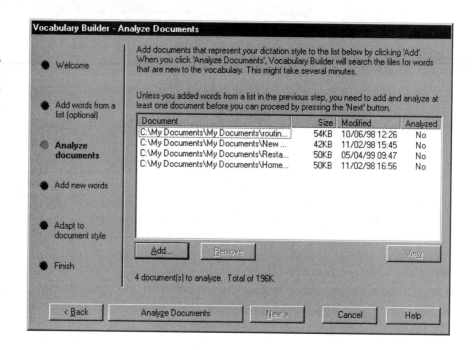

Click the Open button to add your selections to the list of documents to be processed (Figure 14-4). To choose more files for the document list, click the Add button again.

NaturallySpeaking will take from 2 to 20 minutes or more to complete processing, depending upon the speed of your computer, the file formats used, and the number of files.

Choose New Words to Add

When the program finishes processing, it displays a list of all words in all processed documents that it didn't find in its active or backup vocabularies (Figure 14-5).

Figure 14-5
Check off any words
you wish to add.
Click Add Checked
Words to Vocabulary
if you did check off
any words. Then
click Next.

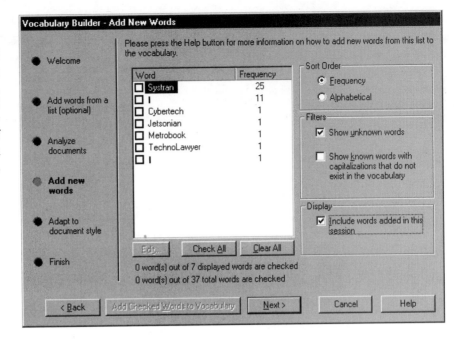

Read through the list and check off any new words to be added to your vocabulary. Ignore (don't check off) words that are misspelled. Proper names are the most common type of new word to add. Focus on the words toward the top of the frequency list—don't bother adding words you seldom say. Most people find fewer than 20 words they want to add.

If you did check off any words, click Add Checked Words to Vocabulary. Click Next to continue. On the next screen (Figure 14-6), most people should answer "Yes" to both questions. Read the sidebar below, "Adapt to Document Style," to be sure. Click Next for a summary screen, then Finish to finish improving your vocabulary. You should now experience better accuracy whenever you dictate text similar to the sample documents the program processed.

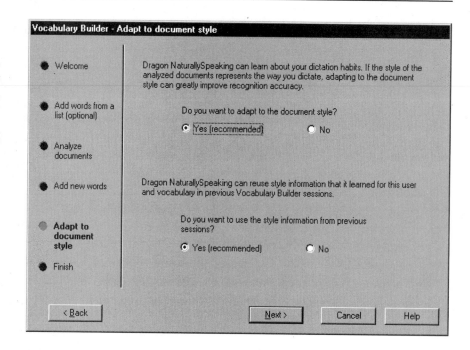

Figure 14-6
See the sidebar "Adapt to Document Style" for an explanation of this screen.

Adapt to Document Style

The Vocabulary Builder asks two questions about how to use the documents you're instructing it to process. Both questions are shown in Figure 14-6.

The top questions asks, essentially, "Are the documents you've given me typical of your normal dictation?" Most people will answer this question "Yes."

The one exception is if you want NaturallySpeaking to add new words only, ignoring writing style. For example, suppose you want to teach NaturallySpeaking the names and address you use most. Process a list of names and addresses with the Vocabulary Builder. In this case, you would want NaturallySpeaking to learn all the names, but ignore the writing style (you're giving it a list of addresses, not the sort of complete sentences you typically dictate.). In this case, you would answer "No" to that top question.

The bottom question asks, "Should I add these new documents to what I already know about how you write?" In most cases, you want NaturallySpeaking to keep all the information it already has about your dictation style, *plus* learn from the new documents you're processing. Answer "Yes" to this question.

The exception is when you want to NaturallySpeaking to forget all the writing style information it knows. For example, suppose you've been dictating financial reports. Then you decide to pack in your office job for the life of a novelist. You have 20 short stories and drafts on disk. You want NaturallySpeaking to forget what it knows about financial reports and learn to expect your fiction writing instead. To do this, run Vocabulary Builder and process those 20 short story files, answering "No" to this question.

Find New Words

Occasionally you'll want to teach NaturallySpeaking new words without having the program learn from the context of how the words appear. For example, you might want to teach Naturally-Speaking the names in a list of addresses. The Vocabulary Builder can do this, but the command Find New Words is simpler.

Display your address list (or other file with new words) in the NaturallySpeaking window. To do this most easily, open the file in another program, copy the text, and paste it into Naturally-Speaking. Check off any words to add and click Add Checked Words to Vocabulary, as in the instructions for the Vocabulary Builder (Figure 14-5 above).

Adding a List of Words

With an option in the Vocabulary Builder, you can add to your vocabulary a list of words, phrases, and words which have different spoken and written forms. This can be useful for adding people's names, if you want the first and last name to be added together as the same phrase, improving accuracy. You could also add a list of e-mail addresses, where the spoken form of the e-mail address would be different from what gets typed out.

You can add a list of words from any text (.txt) file. All word processors can save files in this format. You can also create a text file by starting a new document in NaturallySpeaking, entering the words and phrases to add, then saving the file in text format.

In the text file, each word or phrase should be on a separate line. To add spoken forms that are different from written forms, type the written form, then a backslash, then the spoken form. Your file might look like this:

Christopher Donnelly
Tara Koslov
Bureau of Labor Statistics\B. L. S.

pete31@SayICan.com\Pete e-mail address
abracadabra

To add these words and phrases to your vocabulary, choose Vocabulary Builder from the NaturallySpeaking Tools menu. Follow the on-screen instructions, as described in the section above. On the page titled "Add Words from a List", enter the name of the text file you created, then click the button "Add Words from List" (Figure 14-1). Continue through the Vocabulary Builder, and NaturallySpeaking will add your new words and phrases automatically.

Multiple Vocabularies

If you dictate technical reports by day but moonlight as a novelist, you'll get best accuracy by creating a separate vocabulary for each type of writing. With multiple vocabularies, you can change vocabularies on the fly, whenever you change the type of document you're writing. The words and frequency information for each vocabulary are different, but the acoustical information (your pronunciations) stay the same. Shorthands you've created are specific to each vocabulary, but macros are available in all vocabularies for a particular user.

Separate vocabularies are available only in NaturallySpeaking Professional, Medical, and Legal editions. For other editions, you can create multiple users, which is less convenient. By creating another user, NaturallySpeaking treats you as a different person, and you'll need to retrain your voice files from the beginning. To create a new user, choose New from the User menu.

To create a new vocabulary, choose New from the Vocabulary menu. Type a name for your vocabulary and choose what language model it will use from the Based On drop-down list, as shown in Figure 14-8.

Figure 14-8
Type a name and
choose what
language model it
should be based on.

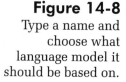

New Vocabulary

Vocabulary name:
fiction writing

Based on:
Base General English - BestMatch

OK

Cancel

Help

For the Professional edition, Base General English - BestMatch is usually the best choice. Base General English - BestMatch 64k+ uses a larger active vocabulary. This can give better accuracy for large-vocabulary writing, but requires more RAM. For best performance, choose this option only if you have at least 96 MB of RAM.

Vocabularies you've created are listed at the bottom of the Vocabulary menu in NaturallySpeaking. Choose the vocabulary you want from the menu to load it into memory. You can also change vocabularies by choosing Open from the Vocabulary menu. To make NaturallySpeaking start with a specific vocabulary loaded, see "Shortcut to a Vocabulary," page 220.

You can share vocabulary information with other users by exporting a vocabulary to disk, then having the other user import it. From the Vocabulary Menu choose Open, then press the Export or Import button and follow the on-screen instructions.

Medical and Legal Editions

The Dragon Medical and Legal Suites consist of NaturallySpeaking Professional plus a medical or legal vocabulary, installed from a separate CD. If you've installed a medical or legal vocabulary, this vocabulary will be available in the Based On menu (Figure 14-8). If you'll be dictating only medical reports, you need only one vocabulary based on the medical language model. If you'll be dictating both medical reports and, say, personal correspondence, use two vocabularies, one based on the medical language model and the other based on Base General English - BestMatch.

Training Words and Commands

Use Training to teach NaturallySpeaking how you speak. This is most useful when NaturallySpeaking repeatedly misrecognizes a word, phrase, or command. Words, shorthands, dictation commands, and other commands are trained in different places within NaturallySpeaking.

Words and Phrases

Train a word or phrase if correcting it in the Correction window still does not make NaturallySpeaking recognize it accurately. To train a word or phrase, choose Train Words from the Naturally-Speaking Tools menu (Figure 14-9).

Figure 14-9
Type the word and
click OK.

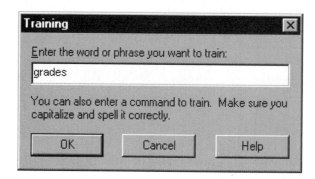

Type the word or phrase and click OK (or say "Click OK"). In the next dialog box (Figure 14-10), click Record (or say "Click Record").

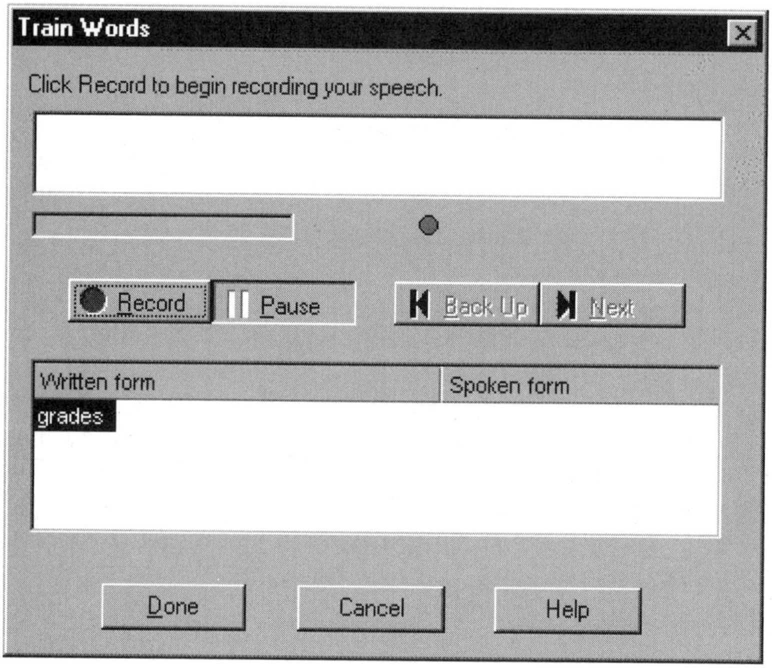

Figure 14-10
Click Record and
say the word to
train it.

NaturallySpeaking will ask you to pronounce the word once. It should now recognize this word more accurately. Like other changes, training for words is not permanently saved until you save your speech files.

Alternatively, you can train words in the Vocabulary Editor. Choose Vocabulary Editor from the Tools menu. Select the word or phrase to train and click the Train button.

Shorthands

Train shorthands in the Vocabulary Editor. Choose Vocabulary Editor from the Tools menu, select the shorthand to train, and click the Train button.

Dictation Commands and Punctuation

Fourteen special dictation commands, when misrecognized, must be trained in the Vocabulary Editor. These commands are the few that can be said in the middle of a sentence, such as "Caps On." To see these commands and train them, choose Vocabulary Editor from the Tools menu. Scroll the word list all the way to the top (Figure 14-11). Select the command that NaturallySpeaking is misrecognizing and click Train.

Figure 14-11
The first eleven dictation commands.

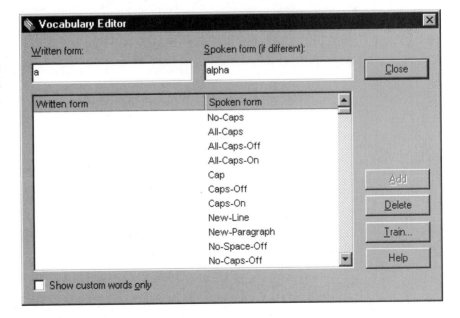

The dictation commands are No-Space, No-Space-On, No-Space-Off, All-Caps, All-Caps-On, All-Caps-Off, Cap, Caps-On, Caps-Off, No-Caps, No-Caps-On, No-Caps-Off, New-Line, and New-Paragraph.

To train punctuation, scroll down just past the dictation commands shown in Figure 14-11. Select the punctuation mark you want and click Train.

Other Commands and Macros

To train macros and all commands except the fourteen dictation commands, use the Train Words command from the Tools menu, just like training a word or phrase. Type the command with proper capitalization and spelling (Figure 14-12). All built-in commands in NaturallySpeaking have initial capital letters.

Figure 14-12
Type the command
with proper
capitalization and
click OK.

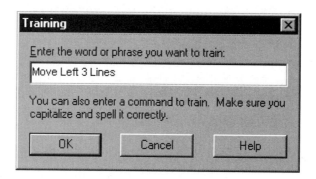

Train macros the same way, by typing the macro name in the Train Words dialog box and clicking OK.

When Training Doesn't Fix the Problem

Occasionally you'll train a word, shorthand, or command until your face turns blue, but NaturallySpeaking absolutely refuses to recognize it accurately. As a workaround, create a shorthand that types the same thing. If your NaturallySpeaking edition supports macros, you can also create a "synonym" macro using the script command HeardWord. See Chapter 11 for instructions.

15

Healthy Computing

The best way to stay healthy at your computer is to stay relaxed. Many of us tense up around computers. Cultivating calmness will make your body feel good.

Equally important is choosing the right equipment and positioning it to fit your body. Your keyboard, mouse, monitor, and chair should be set up to cause minimal strain.

Voice care is also vital. Radio announcers and disc jockeys depend on their voices for their livelihood. Using speech recognition, you're also depending on your voice.

Equipment

Creating a comfortable work station is well worth an investment of time and money. You probably already have a chair, keyboard, and mouse—but do they help or hurt your body? Equipment choices are quite personal. What one person likes another will find unusable. Try several devices—over a few days, if possible—and choose based on comfort. For more information on the products listed here, see Chapter 20, "Resources."

Chairs

A comfortable, adjustable office chair lasts many years and can prevent or lessen back pain. Look for a chair that adjusts in height and swivels, and that has a tilting back and seat. Adjustments let you vary your posture as you work, so you're not stuck in a fixed position all the time. The back of the chair should extend high enough to support the upper part of your back and low enough to support your lower back.

Keyboards

Several alternative keyboards are available that offer different shapes and key configurations. Manufacturers claim that typing on their keyboards strain the hands less than the traditional flat keyboard. Many speech recognition users find that they type relatively little, however, and do fine with standard keyboards. If you are considering buying an alternative keyboard, be sure to try it out before purchase.

Mice and Other Pointing Devices

If you prefer a traditional mouse, find one that requires a light touch on its mouse buttons. Many users report that pressing the mouse button causes more discomfort than either moving the mouse or typing. Other pointing devices available include:

- ▶ Trackballs. Most trackballs feature a ball the size of a pool ball set in a recessed box. To move the pointer, roll the ball with your fingertips or palm. To click, press buttons, like a mouse. Kensington makes a popular trackball of this type. Another manufacturer, Logitech, makes trackballs with a walnut-sized ball you roll with your thumb. The Microsoft EasyBall, designed for children, is a bright yellow trackball a bit larger than a grapefruit. Some adults with limited hand use prefer this device.
- ▶ Touch pads. Touch pads, pressure-sensitive rectangles, are found on many laptops. They are available as external

pointing devices for desktops as well. Slide one finger on the pad to move the pointer. Click by gently tapping your finger on the pad. This is the only type of pointing device that doesn't require pressing buttons to click—instead you tap on the pad with a very light touch. Glidepoint pads from Cirque, such as their Power Cat model, work especially well.

▶ Foot mouse. To use the No-Hands Mouse from Hunter Digital, rest your feet atop its two oval pedals. Swivel one foot to move the pointer, and use your other foot to click. This pointing device is a viable option for people with little or no hand use. People who are able to use a hand-operated device tend to find the foot mouse cumbersome.

▶ Foot control pedals. Step-On-It pedals from Bilbo Innovations let you press keys, enter key sequences, or click the mouse by pressing one of three pedals. You still need a mouse or other pointing device to move the cursor.

Ergonomics and Posture

Good ergonomics—setting up your equipment to properly fit your body—are essential for healthy computing. Adjusting your monitor or keyboard even an inch or two can make a big difference by reducing tension in your neck, shoulders, and hands. If you're already experiencing pain or discomfort while typing, consult a qualified health professional.

When adjusting your workstation, comfort should be your main guide. The suggestions that follow work for most people. However, it's your body that ultimately signals the best arrangement for your workstation.

A good ergonomic setup for speech recognition is the same as a good setup for typing. Set your chair height so that your feet are flat on the ground and your hips are an inch or two above your knees. If the chair is the proper height, your body weight will be supported partly by your feet and partly by the chair seat.

If the keyboard is at the ideal height, the angle of your elbows while typing should be slightly more open than 90 degrees. The mouse or other pointing device should be at the same height as the keyboard.

Place the monitor so that the top of the screen is an inch or two above eye level. With this positioning, you can look straight ahead to see the first line of type in your document and read the rest of the screen by moving your eyes down—moving the whole head is not necessary.

Also make sure that no light sources are reflected in the monitor. If there are windows in the same room as the computer, it's usually best to place the monitor at a right angle to the windows.

Problems and Solutions

If your monitor and keyboard are both sitting on the desktop, the keyboard is probably way too high and the monitor too low. A variety of monitor stands are available from office supply stores and catalogs. For a low-cost solution, stack reams of copy paper under the monitor.

Lowering the height of the keyboard usually requires installing a keyboard tray. Fully adjustable keyboard trays can run $200 or more. Less expensive, less adjustable models from Rubbermaid and other manufacturers are available from office supply stores. Look for a tray with room for the mouse as well as the keyboard. Most models attach with screws to the underside of the desk. Though expensive, a good keyboard tray can make a big difference in comfort and preventing injury. In the meantime, try typing with the keyboard on your lap.

Even for people who use speech recognition, keyboard height is important. Most speech recognition users find themselves typing at times.

If your desk cannot accommodate a keyboard tray, the best solution is raising your chair height so that your elbow angle is a bit more open than 90 degrees. At this chair height, your feet may dangle off the ground—you'll need a foot rest so you can place your feet on a flat surface. Adjustable foot rests are available, but a sturdy box of the right height works well too. If you raise your chair height, of course, raise your monitor height also.

Laptop computers, unmodified, are ergonomically terrible. Placed on a table or desk, the keyboard is too high, the monitor is too low, and the pointing devices are small and awkward to use. Have an external monitor, keyboard, and mouse at each location you use the computer frequently (say, home and office). If this is not possible, at least have an external keyboard at each location. Standard keyboards cost $25 or less. Put the laptop on a monitor stand, box, or stack of paper so that the top of the laptop screen is at eye level. Use the external keyboard and an external mouse in a keyboard tray. If you don't have a keyboard tray, try using the keyboard on your lap.

Maintaining Good Vocal Health

Some people experience vocal strain when using speech recognition software. Like an athlete stretching before a run, you can take preventative measures to maintain good vocal health.

Speak Normally, with These Guidelines

▶ Speak in a relaxed matter, approximating your normal flow of speech.

▶ Use pitch and inflection. There's no need to speak in a monotone. You'll put much more energy into your voice this way, which is healthier for you and makes Naturally-Speaking more accurate.

▶ Speaking well has an open feeling to it, like the feeling inside right before a yawn. This open sense, which has been described as an "inner smile," makes for sound, comfortable speaking.

▶ Breathe with the diaphragm, rather than more shallowly, in the chest, to better support your voice.

Notice Your Breathing

Put your hand on your belly. If you're breathing through your diaphragm, your hand will rise (your belly will expand) as you inhale. As you exhale, your hand will fall. Breathing this way may take some practice, but it's well worth getting into the habit.

If you're breathing from the chest, your chest will rise and fall instead of your belly.

Ease and Comfort

▶ If you typically make hand gestures as you speak to other people in person, go ahead and make those gestures at the computer. Your voice will have more energy, and speaking will be more relaxed and comfortable.

▶ Vary your posture. Don't just sit and dictate—stand up at your computer, or pace around (as your microphone cord allows). Wireless microphones can give you even more pacing room. One of the benefits of speech recognition is that you're not stuck in a frozen, rigid posture at the keyboard.

Taking Care of Yourself

- ▶ Ease into it. Start using NaturallySpeaking for 30 minutes a day, gradually increasing to several hours a day over the course of two to three weeks. This gives your body the opportunity to adapt gradually to speaking to the computer.
- ▶ When dictating, take frequent breaks—at least 10 minutes each hour is best. This is excellent advice for typing as well.
- ▶ Vary your work. Don't dictate for eight hours straight. If you can, vary your work—perhaps two hours of dictation in the morning, then two in the afternoon, with paperwork, phone calls, and typing in the middle.
- ▶ Avoid dictating to NaturallySpeaking when you're tired. This strains your voice and makes it difficult to get good recognition.

Your Vocal Folds

As you speak, your vocal folds vibrate and rub against each other. A layer of mucus liberates them and keeps them from getting irritated.

- ▶ Drink lots of water. Room temperature water is best. Drinking water creates more mucus on your vocal folds (and that's a good thing). The water you drink now will take about four hours to create more mucus—start drinking early in the day.
- ▶ Caffeine and alcohol dehydrate your body, so they're not good for your voice.
- ▶ Certain vocal exercises, similar to the ones that singers use, can help warm up your voice. They are difficult to demonstrate on paper, however. Contact a vocal coach or singing teacher for instruction.

Voice Problems

Occasionally speech recognition users find that the increased use of their voice creates hoarseness or other voice trouble. If this happens to you routinely, give your voice and software a rest and consult a speech therapist or other qualified professional. Consulting with a speech therapist is typically effective in these cases and often leads people to discover and solve general problems in using their voices. The best way to find a qualified professional in your area is through personal recommendations—from physicians, friends, associates, or a local voice software vendor.

Happily, speaking in a way that is good for your voice will also bring you the highest recognition accuracy. This feeds back on itself. Speaking in a clear, relaxed way will bring more accuracy, which brings less frustration, which helps you relax.

Pay attention to what conditions are present when your speech is transcribed well and when NaturallySpeaking makes many errors. This feedback from the computer can encourage you to be more relaxed and more articulate.

16

Using the Dragon NaturallyMobile Recorder

Dictating into a portable recorder frees you from having to sit in front of the computer as you write. You can dictate into the recorder anytime, anywhere. When you return to the computer, NaturallySpeaking transcribes what you said. You can even use the Dragon NaturallyMobile recorder as a hand-held microphone while it's attached to the computer.

If you have the Dragon NaturallyMobile recorder (also known as the Voice It recorder), this chapter is for you. It explains how to set up the NaturallyMobile recorder, how to speak to it for best accuracy, and how to transcribe the recordings you've made. If you have a different recorder model, turn to Chapter 17, "Using Other Recorders."

Using the NaturallyMobile recorder is a two-part process. First, you train NaturallySpeaking to recognize your voice as it sounds using microphone in the recorder. Then, once initial training is complete, you can dictate to the recorder and have NaturallySpeaking transcribe your dictation. These two steps are the same, conceptually, as when you first set up Naturally-Speaking to recognize your speech through a microphone, though a few details are different in practice.

How NaturallySpeaking Hears a Recording

The NaturallyMobile recorder records sound information digitally. As you speak, it convert the sound of your voice to numbers, which are stored in the recorder's memory as a numerical, digital file. You use a special software program called the Voice It Link, included with the recorder, to transfer the file to NaturallySpeaking through a serial port on your computer.

Recorder Setup

If you're familiar with connecting equipment to your computer, the setup instructions here should be sufficient to get you up and running quickly. If you need more detail, see the instructions included with your recorder for additional help.

Here are the key steps in setting up the NaturallyMobile recorder, followed by more detail about each step.

1. Turn on the recorder, make a test recording of a sentence or two, and play it back, so that you hear your recorded voice through the recorder's speaker.
2. Plug the recorder connector cable into one of the serial ports on your computer (make sure the computer is off when you do this).
3. Plug the other end of the cable into the recorder.
4. Install the Voice It Link software if it's not installed.
5. Confirm that the link software can connect to the recorder.
6. Play back your test recording through the computer's speakers, to confirm that everything is set up properly.

First, record a few sentences with the recorder and play them back, so that you hear your voice through the recorder's speaker. You may need to adjust the volume dial on the recorder.

Second, turn off your computer and plug the recorder connector cable into a free serial port.

Third, plug the other end of the connector cable into the bottom of the recorder. (This connector looks like a USB connector, but it actually plugs into the recorder, not the computer's USB port.)

Fourth, check that the Voice It Link software is installed. From the Windows Start menu, go to Programs and look in the Dragon NaturallySpeaking group. You should see "Voice It Link" as an item in this group. If you don't see it, install the software that came with your recorder, which includes the Voice It Link.

Fifth, make sure the recorder is off (but not unplugged) and start the Voice It Link program (from the Windows Start menu, in the Dragon NaturallySpeaking group). The Voice It Link program opens. Choose "Link to Recorder" from the program's Link menu. The recorder should turn on automatically. This confirms that the computer and recorder can communicate with each other.

If the Voice It recorder does not turn on, or if you get an on-screen message "Communications Error," the Voice It Link program cannot find the recorder. In this case, choose "Communications Options" from the Link menu, change the "Com Port" setting, and try again. Refer to the recorder's instructions for more details, or consult "Troubleshooting" in the Voice It Link online help.

Sixth, now that the recorder is linked to the computer, you should see a file in the right-hand section of the screen (as in Figure 16-1). This file is the test sentences you recorded.

Figure 16-1
The file you recorded is shown on-screen ("File 01" in this picture).

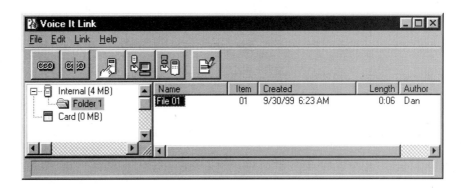

Click once on the file to select it, then choose "Play Recorder File" from the File menu. You should hear your voice through the computer's speakers. (If you can't hear anything when you try this, make sure your speakers are plugged in, turned on, and the volume is turned up.)

Hearing your recorded voice through the computer's speakers conforms that your equipment is set up correctly. Exit the Voice It Link program. You're now ready to proceed to enrollment, where you teach the computer the sound of your voice.

Enrollment

You can transcribe recorded speech using the same speech files you first created by dictating into the headset microphone. Your voice spoken directly to the computer through the headset microphone, though, sounds different than it does when recorded and played back. For better accuracy, set up a new user—separate speech files—for your voice dictated into the recorder. In the NaturallySpeaking window, choose New from the User menu. Label the new user with your name plus the recorder you're using (e.g., "Dan Voice It") to distinguish it from the dictate-directly-to-the-computer user you already have (Figure 16-2).

Figure 16-2
Type the new user name and click Next. For Medical and Legal editions, choose Medical or Legal from the Vocabulary drop down list.

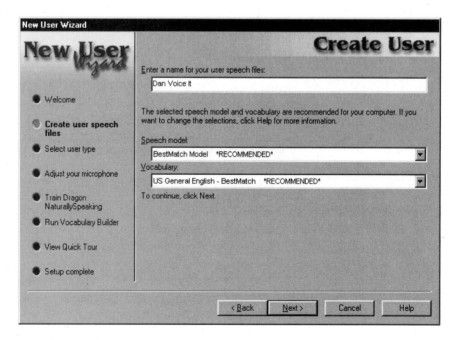

After typing in the name for your new user, click the Next button. In a few moments, NaturallySpeaking will ask you to select a user type. Choose the Into a Recorder option, then the Use the Dragon NaturallyMobile Recorder option, as shown in Figure 16-3.

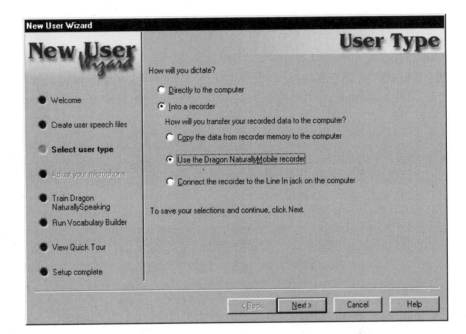

Figure 16-3
Select the options shown and click Next.

Close the Voice It Link program if it's still running. Then click Next and follow the on-screen instructions to begin training. During training, NaturallySpeaking uses the recorder as a handheld microphone. Speak into the recorder's microphone to teach NaturallySpeaking the sound of your voice.

For best accuracy, hold the microphone to the side of your mouth as you speak—don't speak directly into it. The microphone should be about an inch or two away from your mouth.

You'll read to the computer for between 5 and 45 minutes, depending on the speed of your computer. The yellow arrow on the screen shows you what to read. Sometimes the arrow will not move forward as you speak, which means that you need to repeat the words you just read. If this happens three times in a row on the same words, click the Skip Word button to move on.

You can pause to take a break at any time by clicking the Pause button. Click the Record button to resume.

After you've read enough, a message will appear telling you so. Click Finish to complete enrollment. NaturallySpeaking will process your speech files, which takes a few minutes. Your enrollment is now complete.

Speaking to a Recorder

When you speak to the recorder, do so in the same way you speak into a microphone while at the computer. Speak clearly, enunciate, and avoid mumbling. Review Chapter 13 for good speaking tips.

When dictating, keep the recorder's microphone a consistent distance from your mouth. The microphone should be 1 to 2 inches from the corner of your mouth. Place it near the corner of your mouth, not directly in front, to avoid recording noise from your breath.

You'll typically get better transcription accuracy if you use a headset microphone with the recorder. You can plug the headset microphone that came with your software into the Naturally-Mobile unit, bypassing the recorder's built-in mic. A headset microphone keeps the microphone a consistent distance from your mouth, so there's less variability in how your voice sounds to the computer. Alternately, you can use a "stalk" microphone, which sticks out from the recorder like a small mushroom. You can read more about stalk mics online at SayICan.com.

Transcribing from a recorder tends to be less accurate than dictating directly to the computer, for several reasons. Recorder users tend to slur their speech more. Dictating directly, you have immediate feedback on screen. If NaturallySpeaking is making many errors, you can speak more clearly. Dictating to a recorder, though, it's easy to forget that your speech will be transcribed by a computer, and there's a tendency to slip into slurred words and mumbling. For best results, practice dictating directly to the computer before starting to use a recorder. This will help you learn a speaking style that gives the best accuracy.

Also avoidable is the tendency of recorder users to move the microphone around as they speak. This makes your voice vary in quality on the recording, making NaturallySpeaking less accurate. For best results, keep the recorder's built-in microphone in a consistent position relative to your mouth. For even better accuracy, use a headset mic plugged into the recorder.

Transcribing a Recording

Before instructing NaturallySpeaking to transcribe your recorded speech, be sure to choose the correct user—the one trained from the NaturallyMobile unit. You can change users from the NaturallySpeaking Users menu.

To transcribe, start the Voice It Link program and connect to the recorder (choose "Link to Recorder" from the Link menu). In the right-hand section of the screen you'll see a list of files in the recorder's memory (as in Figure 16-1).

To select the file you want to transcribe, click on it. Then choose "Transcribe" from the File menu to begin transcription. The Voice It Link copies the file from the recorder to the computer, then sends it to NaturallySpeaking, which transcribes it automatically.

You can transcribe more than one file at a time. Just select all the files you want before choosing Transcribe. To select multiple files, hold down the Ctrl key as you click on each one. To select a range of files, click on the first file you want, then hold down the Shift key while you click on the last file. NaturallySpeaking transcribes the files unattended, one after the other.

Using the Recorder as a Handheld Microphone

When the NaturallyMobile recorder is plugged in to the computer, you can use it as a handheld microphone. As you speak, the words you say appear the screen immediately, just like using a headset mic. This feature is convenient for editing your transcribed text by voice.

To use your recorder this way, make sure that:

▶ The recorder is plugged in to the connecting cable, which is plugged in to your computer's serial port.
▶ The user open in NaturallySpeaking is the one you created with the NaturallyMobile recorder.
▶ The Voice It Link program is not running.

If all three of these things are true, when you turn the mic on in NaturallySpeaking (such as by pressing the numeric "+" key), you can talk into the recorder's microphone.

If you see an error message like Figure 16-4 when you turn the microphone on, this means that NaturallySpeaking cannot locate the recorder. This could mean that the recorder is not plugged in or not properly configured.

Figure 16-4
If you see this message, check that the recorder is plugged in.

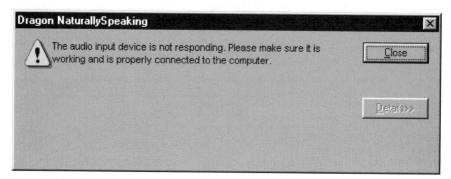

Dragon On-Screen Recorder

Included with NaturallySpeaking is the Dragon Sound Recorder, software that lets your PC work like a digital tape recorder. You can dictate to the Sound Recorder, saving your file for later transcription.

If you're using a computer that has NaturallySpeaking on it, it's more practical to dictate directly to NaturallySpeaking than into the on-screen recorder. Dictating to NaturallySpeaking, you can see your words instantly on screen, which is much more convenient. If you're using a computer without NaturallySpeaking, though, you can save your recorded files and move them to the NaturallySpeaking computer for later transcription. This could be particularly useful on a computer that is too slow or has too little memory to run NaturallySpeaking.

To use the Sound Recorder, from the Windows Start menu, choose Programs, Dragon NaturallySpeaking, Sound Recorder. The recorder appears on screen (see Figure 17-12, page 210). For more details and instructions, press F1 for help while the Sound Recorder is displayed.

17

Using Other Recorders

Dictating into a portable recorder frees you from having to sit in front of the computer as you write. You can dictate into the recorder anytime, anywhere. When you return to the computer, NaturallySpeaking transcribes what you said.

If you have the Dragon NaturallyMobile recorder (also known as the Voice It recorder), read Chapter 16, which is specific to that recorder. If you have any other recorder, this chapter is for you.

How NaturallySpeaking Hears a Recording

NaturallySpeaking hears what you said in one of two ways—through the sound card or by digital transfer. When speaking directly to the computer through a microphone, the microphone transmits electrical signals to the computer's sound card, which converts the signals into numbers for NaturallySpeaking to process. Instead of using a microphone, you can play a tape recording to the sound card, and NaturallySpeaking will transcribe it. NaturallySpeaking is fooled into thinking that you're dictating when you're actually playing back a recording.

Some recorders can transfer sound information digitally. In this case, sound is converted into numbers by the recorder, not the sound card. These numbers are stored in the recorder as a numerical, digital file, then transferred to NaturallySpeaking. This file is transferred through the serial, parallel, USB, or PC-card port on your computer—the particular port used depends on the model of the recorder. Special link software running on your computer allows it to connect to the recorder and transfer the file. Digital recorders store sound in a compressed format to save memory. After moving the compressed file to your computer, the link software will convert it to ".wav" format, the standard file format that NaturallySpeaking uses to transcribe.

Two Types of Sound Recording

Cassette recorders store sound in analog form, as wave patterns on tape. Digital recorders (tapeless voicemail systems, for example) store sound as a group of numbers. All recorders, analog and digital, can play sound to NaturallySpeaking through the sound card. Most digital recorders can also transfer sound to NaturallySpeaking digitally. If your recorder allows it, always transfer sound digitally for the best transcription accuracy.

Recorder type	Examples	Sound can be transferred	
		Through sound card	Digitally
Analog	Norcom minicassette	Yes	No
	Philips minicassette	Yes	No
Digital	Sony Minidisc	Yes	No
	Voice It/Dragon NaturallyMobile recorder	Yes	Yes
	Olympus D1000	Yes	Yes

Which Recorder Should I Use?

You'll need a recorder specifically designed to work with speech recognition. Other recorders tend to distort speech too much in recording or are unable to convey sound faithfully to the computer. The most important characteristics of a recorder are the quality of its built-in microphone and how accurately it reproduces your voice. Also important is how much dictation it can store on one tape, memory chip, or Minidisc. Digital recorders tend to reproduce sound better than analog, tape-based units. However, some digital recorders have poor built-in microphones, reducing overall accuracy. You can bypass this problem with most recorders by using an external microphone rather than the one built in. Though external mics are less convenient, they are more accurate.

Recorder models change frequently. For up-to-date information and product comparisons, visit SayICan.com.

Recorder Setup

To get started with your recorder, read the section below that applies to your software version and recorder:

▶ Transferring Sound Digitally
▶ Transferring Sound Through the Sound Card

Transferring Sound Digitally

Connect the recorder and install any needed recorder link software according to the recorder's instructions. Some recorders connect to the computer directly through a cable. Other recorders, like the Olympus D1000, store digital files on memory cards. To move a file to the computer, remove the memory card from the recorder and plug it into the appropriate port on the computer.

Confirm that your recorder is set up correctly by dictating a few sentences to it and playing them back. Next, move the recording to your computer's hard drive using the link software included with the recorder. Save it as a .wav file and play it back from the .wav file to confirm it was transferred correctly. You'll need to review the recorder's instructions to do this.

You can transcribe recorded speech using the same speech files you first created by dictating into the headset microphone. Your voice spoken directly to the computer through the headset microphone, though, sounds different than it does when recorded and played back. For better accuracy, set up a new user—separate speech files—for your voice dictated into the recorder. In NaturallySpeaking, choose New from the User menu. Label the new user with your name plus the recorder you're using (e.g., "Dan Olympus") to distinguish it from the dictate-directly-to-the-computer user you already have (Figure 17-1).

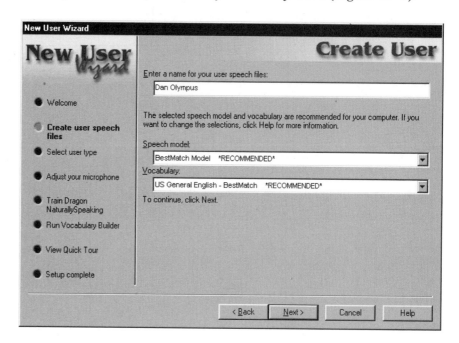

Figure 17-1
Type the new user name and click Next. For Medical and Legal editions, choose Medical or Legal from the Vocabulary drop down list.

After typing in the name for your new user, click the Next button. In a few moments, NaturallySpeaking will ask you to select a user type. Choose the Into a Recorder option, then the Copy the Data From Recorder Memory to the Computer option, and click Next (Figure 17-2).

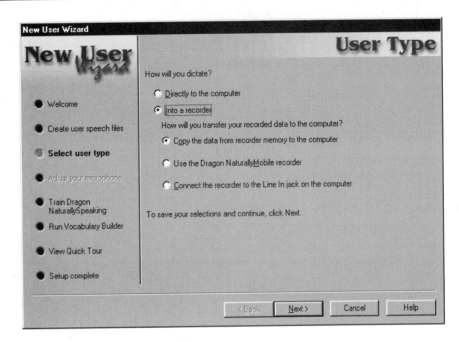

Figure 17-2
Select the options shown and click Next.

The Mobile Recorder Training Wizard appears. Click Next to see a list of training passages to choose from (Figure 17-3).

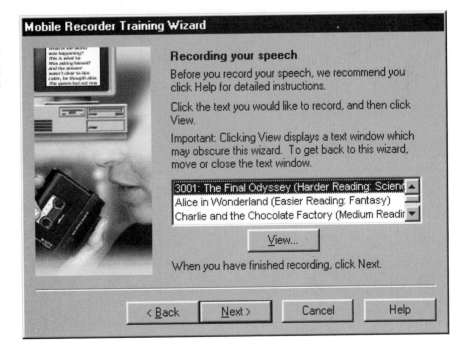

Figure 17-3
Choose the training text you want to read and click View.

Click the title of the text you prefer to read and click View. The text you chose will open in the program Notepad. From the Edit menu in that program, choose Word Wrap to make the text easier to see. Then choose Print from the File menu to print it out, and Exit from the File menu to close (don't save changes). Now you have a printed copy of what to read. (If you don't have a printer, leave the text open in Notepad to read from the screen.)

Review the "Speaking to a Recorder" section below (page 206) for proper microphone positioning. Then turn on the recorder and read the text to it. You don't need to say punctuation, "New Paragraph," or other commands. Just read the text. If you cough or misspeak, it's not necessary to correct it— just keep going. You can stop to take breaks whenever you like.

When you finish reading the text, move the digital file you just recorded from the recorder to the computer's hard drive. Save it as a .wav file. Then click Next (see Figure 17-4).

Figure 17-4
Enter the digital file to be transferred and click Next.

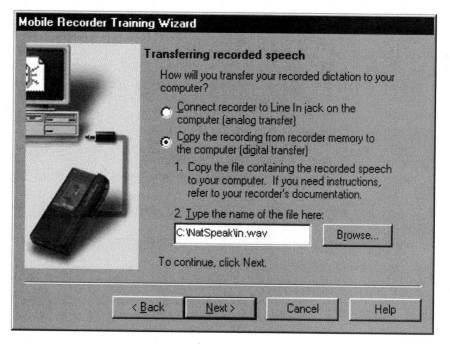

Figure 17-5
Click Start
Adapting.

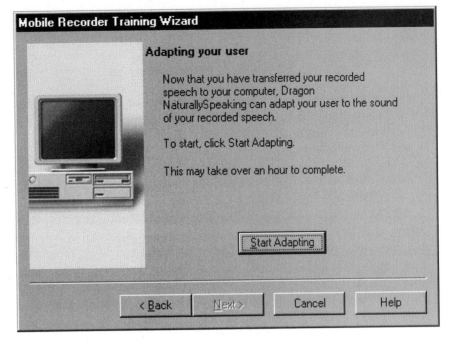

Choose the Copy the Recording from Recorder Memory... option as shown above. Type the name of the .wav file, then click Next. On the next screen (Figure 17-5), click Start Adapting.

NaturallySpeaking will process your recorded voice to create a set of speech files. Depending on your computer and voice, this can take over an hour. Don't use the computer for other tasks while NaturallySpeaking is processing. When NaturallySpeaking has finished, it will ask you to press Next to continue. Click Next, then Finish to complete your new user files.

Keep your recorded digital file on the hard drive or a Zip disk in case you want to set up your voice file on another computer in the future.

Transferring Sound Through the Sound Card

Follow the instructions included with your recorder to connect it properly to your computer. In most cases, a cable will extend from the recorder's ear jack to the sound card's line in jack (which is next to the place where the headset mic is usually plugged in). Sound cards have up to four jacks: mic, line in, speaker out, and line out. Some recorder models connect through a filter box first (these models include a filter box with the recorder). Set the recorder volume as indicated in the recorder instructions.

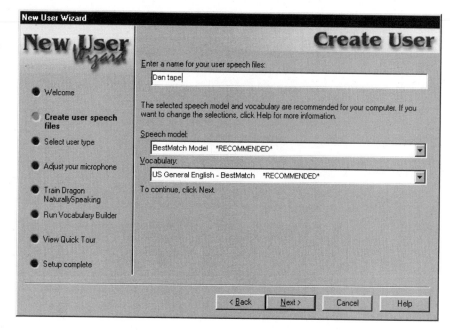

Figure 17-6
Type the new user name and click Next. For Medical and Legal editions, choose Medical or Legal from the Vocabulary drop down list.

You can transcribe recorded speech using the same speech files you first created by dictating into the headset microphone. Your voice spoken directly to the computer through the headset microphone, though, sounds different than it does when recorded and played back. For better accuracy, set up a new user—a separate speech file—for your voice dictated into the recorder. In NaturallySpeaking, choose New from the User menu. Label the new user with your name plus the recorder you're using (e.g., "Dan tape") to distinguish it from the dictate-directly-to-the-computer user you already have (Figure 17-6).

After typing in the name for your new user, click Next. In a few moments, NaturallySpeaking will ask you to select a user type (Figure 17-7).

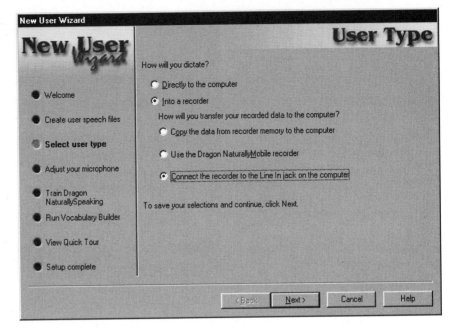

Figure 17-7
Select the options shown and click Next.

Choose the Into a Recorder option and the Connect the Recorder to the Line In jack on the Computer option.

Click Next for the next screen. Run the Audio Setup wizard and follow the on-screen instructions. The Audio Setup wizard will ask you to record, then play back, a test passage of about a minute to set the volume, then it will ask you to record and play back another passage to test sound quality.

Click Next when audio setup is complete to return to the New User Wizard. Click Run Training Program. The Mobile Recorder Training Wizard appears. Click Next to see a list of training passages to choose from (Figure 17-8).

Figure 17-8
Choose the training text you want to read and click View.

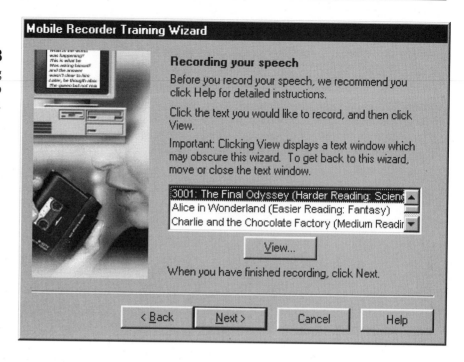

Click the title of the text you prefer to read and click View. The text you chose will open in the program Notepad. From the Edit menu in that program, choose Word Wrap to make the text easier to see. Then choose Print from the File menu to print it out, and Exit from the File menu to close (don't save changes). Now you have a printed copy of what to read. (If you don't have a printer, leave the text open in Notepad to read from the screen.)

Review the "Speaking to a Recorder" section below (page 206) for proper microphone positioning. Then turn on the recorder and read the text to it. You don't need to say punctuation, new paragraph, or other commands. Just read the text. If you cough or misspeak, it's not necessary to correct it— just keep going. You can stop to take breaks whenever you like. If you reach the end of the tape, flip it over and keep going.

When you're finished reading, rewind the tape or disc to the start of the training passage (*not* the start of the volume test passage). Click Next (see Figure 17-9).

Figure 17-9
Choose the option
shown and click
Next.

Choose the Connect Recorder to Line In Jack... option as shown above. Click Next (see Figure 17-10).

Figure 17-10
Be sure the Detect...
checkbox is not
checked before you
click Start
Recording.

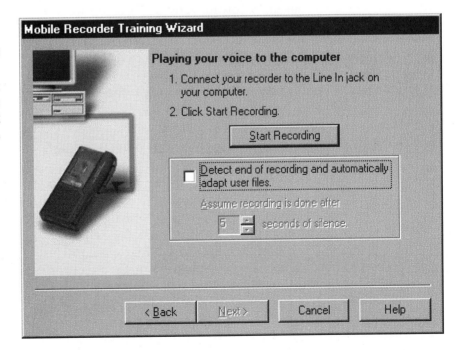

Uncheck the Detect End of Recording... checkbox, click Start Recording, and press play on the recorder to play your recorded voice to NaturallySpeaking. (On most systems you'll hear your voice through the speakers as NaturallySpeaking listens to it. Feel free to turn the volume down or off with the volume control knob on your speakers.)

As NaturallySpeaking listens, the message "Speech Recorded" will appear, along with a clock showing the amount of speech NaturallySpeaking has heard. This clock moves only when NaturallySpeaking hears speech. If the clock is not moving at all or does not appear within the first minute of playback, something is wrong with your training setup.

When the first side of the tape is finished, flip the tape over if there's more of your speech to train. While the tape is playing you can leave the computer unattended.

When the whole training recording is finished playing back, click Next, then Finish. NaturallySpeaking will process your recorded voice into a set of speech files. Depending on your computer and voice, this can take over an hour. Don't use the computer for other tasks while NaturallySpeaking is processing.

Your new user is now complete. Label the tape or disc you used "Training" and set it aside in case you want to set up your voice file on another computer in the future.

Speaking to a Recorder

Speak into the recorder the same way you speak into the microphone while at the computer. Speak clearly, enunciate, and avoid mumbling. Review Chapter 13 for good speaking tips.

When dictating, keep the recorder's microphone a consistent distance from your mouth. For most recorders, the microphone should be 1 to 2 inches from the corner of your mouth. Place it near the corner of your mouth, not directly in front, to avoid recording noise from your breath. Also review the instructions that came with your recorder.

You'll typically get better transcription accuracy if you use a headset microphone with the recorder. You can plug the headset microphone that came with your software into most recorders, bypassing the recorder's built-in mic. A headset microphone keeps the microphone a consistent distance from your mouth, so there's less variability in how your voice sounds to Naturally-

Speaking. Alternately, you can use an add-on "stalk" microphone, which sticks out from the recorder like a small mushroom. You can read more about stalk microphones online at SayICan.com.

Transcribing from a recorder tends to be less accurate than dictating directly to the computer, for several reasons. The sound quality of recorded speech is never quite as good as speech dictated directly, and this adversely affects accuracy. This is an unavoidable consequence of portability.

More easily avoidable is the tendency of recorder users to slur their speech. Dictating directly, you have immediate feedback on screen. If NaturallySpeaking is making many errors, you can speak more clearly. Dictating to a recorder, though, it's easy to forget that your speech will be transcribed by a computer, and there's a tendency to slip into slurred words and mumbling. For best results, practice dictating directly to the computer before starting to use a recorder. This will help you learn a speaking style that gives the best accuracy.

Also avoidable is the tendency of recorder users to move the microphone around as they speak. This makes your voice vary in quality on the recording, making NaturallySpeaking less accurate. Keep the recorder's built-in microphone in a consistent position relative to your mouth for best results. For even better accuracy, use a headset mic plugged into the recorder.

Transcribing a Recording

Before instructing NaturallySpeaking to transcribe your recorded speech, be sure to choose the correct user—the one trained from your voice recorded on that recorder. Change users from the NaturallySpeaking Users menu.

Next, choose Transcribe from the NaturallySpeaking Tools menu (Figure 17-11).

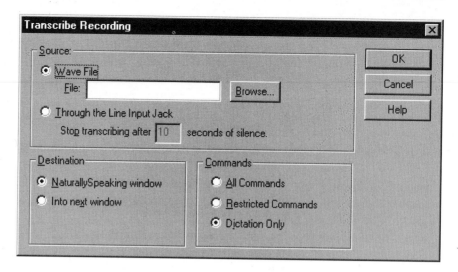

Figure 17-11
The options for transcribing a recording.

To transcribe a digital file, click Wave File as the recording source, as shown. Then click Browse and select the .wav file to transcribe. Sound files must be in standard .wav format. (Technical specifications for this format are PCM 11,025 Hz, 16-bit mono.)

To transcribe through the sound card instead, click Through the Line Input Jack as the recording source. Also enter the amount of silence on the recording before NaturallySpeaking stops transcribing. Ten seconds is usually sufficient. If you have long pauses in your dictation, change this number to 30 or 60.

In the Destination box, choose whether your dictation will be typed into the NaturallySpeaking window or into the next application window open. For best performance, always transcribe into the NaturallySpeaking window. When transcription has finished, copy and paste the text into any program you like.

Next, choose what commands NaturallySpeaking should listen for as it transcribes. For best results, choose Dictation Only, as in Figure 17-11. This prevents dictation from being misrecognized as commands in transcription. The 14 dictation commands, such as Caps-On and New Paragraph, are always active. (See page 178 for a list of these commands.) Changing this setting to Restricted Commands permits NaturallySpeaking to recognize the additional commands Scratch That and Resume With while transcribing.

Finally, click OK to begin transcribing. If you're transcribing through the sound card, press Play on your recorder after clicking OK. Your dictation should begin to appear on screen.

You can use other programs while NaturallySpeaking is transcribing into the NaturallySpeaking window. However, doing this may increase the chance of system resource conflicts, which could decrease accuracy or otherwise reduce system performance.

The Dragon On-Screen Recorder

Included with NaturallySpeaking is the Dragon Sound Recorder, software that lets your PC work like a digital tape recorder. You can dictate to the Sound Recorder, saving your file for later transcription.

If you're using a computer that has NaturallySpeaking on it, it's more practical to dictate directly to NaturallySpeaking than into the on-screen recorder. Dictating to NaturallySpeaking, you can see your words instantly on screen, which is much more convenient. If you're using a computer without NaturallySpeaking, though, you can save your recorded files and move them to the NaturallySpeaking computer for later transcription. This could be particularly useful on a computer that is too slow or has too little memory to run NaturallySpeaking.

To use the Sound Recorder, from the Windows Start menu, choose Programs, Dragon NaturallySpeaking, Sound Recorder. The recorder appears on screen (Figure 17-12).

Figure 17-12
The Dragon
Sound Recorder

Use the six large buttons to record and play back. Choose Save from the File menu to save your recording. For more details and instructions, press F1 for online Help.

18

Customizing NaturallySpeaking

You can customize NaturallySpeaking to make it work better for your needs. The Options dialog box lets you change the spacing after periods, select what key turns the microphone on, and adjust other parts of the software. If more than one person uses NaturallySpeaking on your machine, you can create an icon that starts the program with a particular user's voice file already loaded.

The Options Dialog Box

From the NaturallySpeaking Tools menu, choose Options. The dialog box that opens lets you customize some features of NaturallySpeaking. The box is divided into five tabbed sections: Results Box, Hotkeys, Text-to-Speech, Miscellaneous, and Dictation.

Results Box Options

Figure 18-1 shows the recommended settings for the Results Box tab.

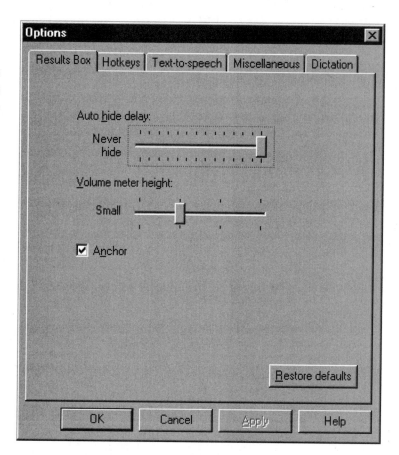

Figure 18-1
The Results Box tab in the Options dialog box.

The Auto Hide Delay control affects how long the Results box stays on the screen after you finish speaking. The far right setting, Never Hide, keeps the Results box on the screen so you can view it easily. Setting the Volume Meter Height control to Small, as shown, lets you see the volume meter color easily but takes up little space on the screen. The Anchor button should be checked so that the Results box stays in the same place on the screen instead of moving as you speak. This makes it easy to glance at as you dictate. Clicking the button Restore Defaults restores the original installation settings.

Hotkey Options

The microphone hot key lets you turn the microphone on and off. You can change it and three other hot keys using this dialog box (Figure 18-2).

Figure 18-2
The Hotkeys tab in the Options dialog box.

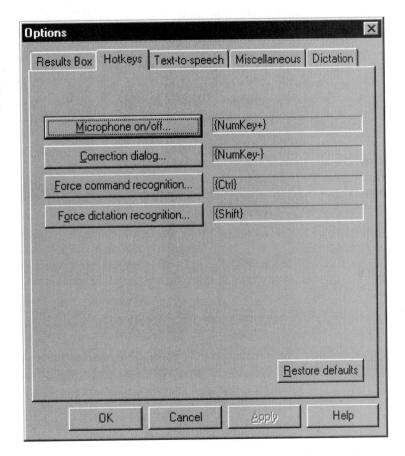

For the Microphone On/Off key, the default (automatically installed) choice of "+" on the numeric keypad is a good one. That key is physically large and easy to find. The Correction Dialog key, which opens the Correction window, has the default setting of "-" on the numeric keypad, which is also a good choice.

To force NaturallySpeaking to recognize what you say as a command, not dictation text, hold down the Ctrl key as you speak. To force NaturallySpeaking to type what you say as dictation (even words that are also commands), hold down the Shift key as you speak. These are the default key settings, and there's no need to change them.

If you have a laptop or if you use a keyboard with no numeric keypad, you should change the hotkeys for Microphone on/off and Correction dialog. Change them to any keys that are easily accessible—try F12 (microphone) and F11 (correction).

To change a hotkey, click on the button with the hotkey's name. A dialog box appears (Figure 18-3). Type the new key and click OK.

Clicking the Restore Defaults button restores the original installation settings.

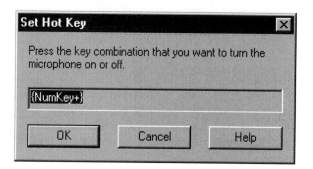

Figure 18-3
Type the key or key combination you want.

Text-to-Speech Options

The Text-to-Speech tab (Figure 18-4) affects how Naturally-Speaking reads text to you in its mechanical voice. See page 144 for instructions on using this feature.

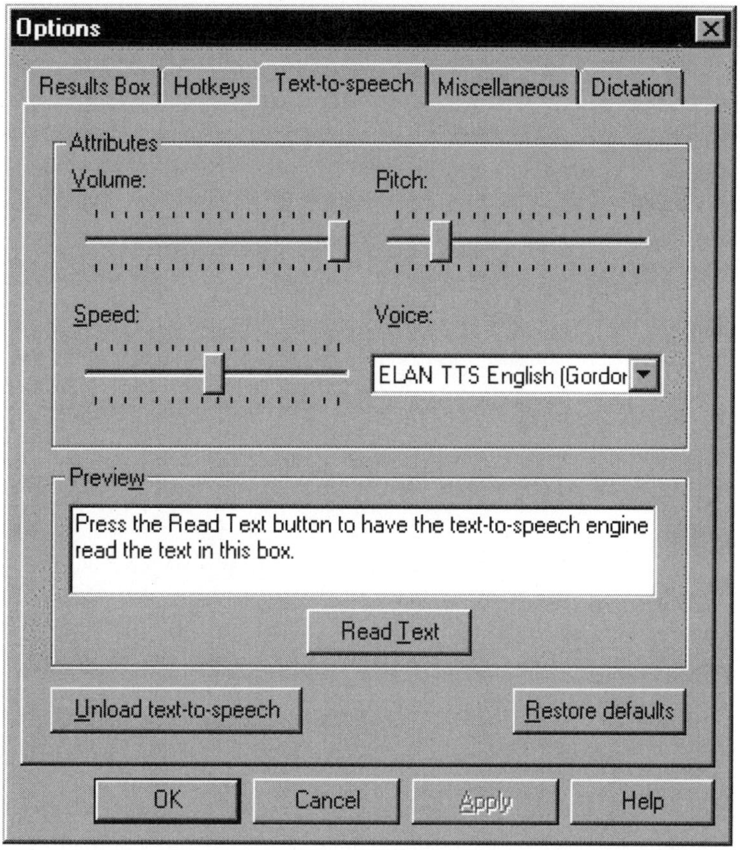

Figure 18-4
The Text-to-Speech
tab in the Options
dialog box.

Move the Volume, Pitch, and Speed controls to change the sound of the computer's voice. Click the Read Text button to have the computer read the text in the Preview box. You can edit the Preview box text if you want to hear the mechanical voice say other words instead, like your name or "I'm stuck inside this computer!"

The Unload Text-to-Speech button lets you temporarily remove this feature from memory. Having text-to-speech loaded does not affect NaturallySpeaking's transcription performance. Clicking the Restore Defaults button restores the original installation settings.

Miscellaneous Options

The Miscellaneous tab controls several unrelated but important settings. Recommended settings are shown in Figure 18-5.

Figure 18-5
The
Miscellaneous tab
in the Options
dialog box.

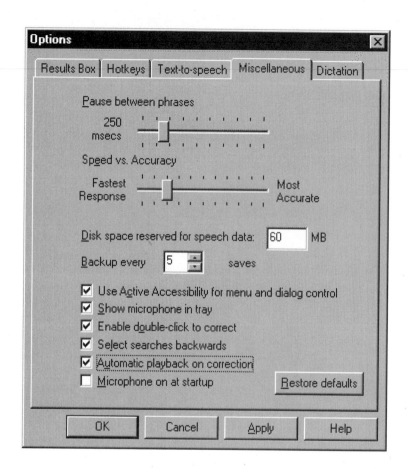

The Pause Between Phrases control affects the length of the pause required before and after commands. Leave this at the default setting of 250 milliseconds. If your commands are being recognized as dictation, or if NaturallySpeaking is not recognizing commands, these problems may be related to pause length. See troubleshooting suggestions in Chapter 21.

The Speed vs. Accuracy control affects how much computer processing NaturallySpeaking uses as it recognizes your speech. The default (automatic) setting varies from computer to computer. For most users, better accuracy is more important than slightly faster recognition. When you begin using Naturally-Speaking, leave this setting at the default. After a few weeks, try moving it one notch to the right. Then spend another week using the software to see if this setting improves accuracy and keeps an acceptable level of speed. Continue making adjustments if you desire. For best results, change the control only a small amount at a time, then use the program for awhile to see if the change makes a difference. On most computers, the default setting or a notch or two to the right of it is best.

The Disk Space Reserved for Speech Data control affects how much disk space NaturallySpeaking uses to record the sound of your voice as you speak. It uses this recording to play back what you said during proofreading and corrections. Unless you are short on disk space, change this setting to 60 MB or higher. One megabyte can store about 48 seconds of sound. To turn off speech recording, change this setting to zero.

The Backup control changes how often NaturallySpeaking backs up your speech files. There's no need to change this control. To back up your speech files more reliably, store them apart from your computer on a Zip disk, tape, or other computer on the same network. See "Backing Up Speech Files," page 164, for backup instructions.

The setting Use Active Accessibility... controls how NaturallySpeaking understands menu names and dialog box controls. Leave this box checked for best results.

Show Microphone in Tray shows a small picture of the microphone in the corner of the screen next to the clock. Leave this setting checked to make the mic easy to turn on and off by mouse (click once on the small mic picture).

Enable Double-Click to Correct brings up the Correction window when you double-click on a word. Start with this control checked and see how it works for you.

Select Searches Backwards makes NaturallySpeaking look backwards in your document when you say "Select" plus some words on the screen. Start with this control checked; change it if you desire.

Automatic Playback on Correction plays your recorded voice through the speakers whenever the Correction window opens. Leave this control checked—hearing your voice played back makes it easier to learn how to speak more clearly and how to correct NaturallySpeaking's mistakes. After becoming familiar with making corrections, you may wish to uncheck this control.

Microphone on at Startup makes NaturallySpeaking start up with the microphone on, but sleeping. This is useful if you have physical limitations that prevent you from using the keyboard or mouse.

The Restore Defaults button restores the original installation settings.

Dictation Options

The Dictation tab (Figure 18-6) controls the spacing after periods and how NaturallySpeaking interprets some spoken commands.

Figure 18-6
The Dictation tab in the Options dialog box.

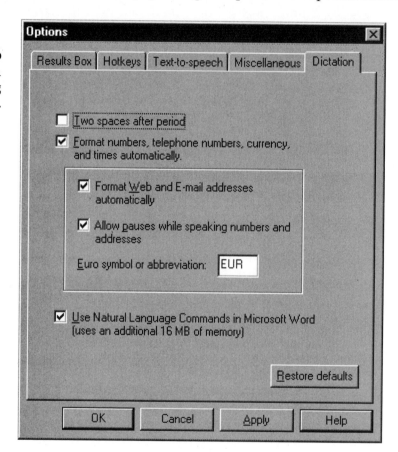

The Two Spaces After Period control puts—you guessed it—two spaces after each period when you dictate. If this box is not checked, NaturallySpeaking types one space. Change this setting as you prefer.

When the Format Numbers... setting and the two settings below it are checked, dictating numbers, web address, and other commonly spoken items is much easier.

The Euro symbol box lets you change what's typed when you say "euro" or "euro sign" during dictation.

The setting Use Natural Language Commands in Microsoft Word controls whether these commands are loaded into memory, using an additional 16 MB of RAM. If you have 64 MB of RAM or less, un-checking this box will probably improve Naturally-Speaking's perfomance in Word. This box is not available if you don't use Word 97 with NaturallySpeaking or if you've created any custom macros.

The Restore Defaults button restores the original installation settings.

Open with a Particular User or Vocabulary

If more than one person uses NaturallySpeaking on the same computer, or if one person has several speech files, Naturally-Speaking will ask which voice file to open each time you start it. You can create a special NaturallySpeaking icon to open a particular user immediately, bypassing NaturallySpeaking's opening question. You can also create a shortcut that loads a particular vocabulary. This saves time if more than one person routinely uses NaturallySpeaking on your computer, or if you often use more than one vocabulary.

Shortcut to a User

To create a shortcut to a particular user on the Windows desktop, follow these steps:

1. Start Windows Explorer. Go to the NatSpeak directory and open the Programs folder. Right-click on the file "Natspeak" and choose Copy. Close Windows Explorer, right-click on the Windows desktop, and choose Paste Shortcut (not Paste). This will create a new icon called Shortcut to Natspeak.

2. Right-click on the icon and choose Properties. Click on the Shortcut tab.

3. In the Target field, add "/user" plus the user name to the end of the field. Leave a space before the slash, a

space after the word "user," and put the name of the user in quotes. The Target field should look like this:

C:\Natspeak.exe /user "Tim Brown"

4. Click OK to finish.

To use the shortcut, double-click on it. NaturallySpeaking will open with that user's voice files loaded. Optionally, you can put the shortcut in the Start menu by dragging it to the Windows Start button.

Shortcut to a Vocabulary

The Deluxe, Professional, Legal, and Medical editions of NaturallySpeaking allow one user to have several vocabularies. You can create an icon that opens NaturallySpeaking automatically to the vocabulary you want. To do this, review the instructions above for creating a shortcut to a user. Instead of adding "/user" in the Target field (step 3, above), add "/vocabulary" plus the name of the vocabulary you want to open. The Target field should look like this:

C:\Natspeak.exe /vocabulary "business writing"

You can specify a user and a vocabulary in the same shortcut. For example:

C:\Natspeak.exe /user "Tim Brown" /vocabulary "business writing"

19

How It Works

People recognize speech effortlessly and automatically. How to reproduce this ability in a computer is a question that has occupied speech researchers for decades. Several advancements have made electronic speech recognition possible: better understanding of sound and language, the development of specialized mathematical techniques, and vast improvements in computer speed and memory.

Many Sources of Knowledge

Alexander Graham Bell tried to make human speech visible back in 1875. His wife, Mabel, had been deaf since age four, and he sought to create a machine that would generate pictures of the different frequencies in speech sounds. Mabel and other deaf people, Bell thought, might be able to understand speech by looking at the graphs drawn by his machine. While experimenting he accidentally connected one of the wires to the wrong part of his apparatus. Sound unexpectedly came out of the microphone—Bell had invented the telephone. Bell did later get his machine to generate sound pictures, but the graphs proved too complex for humans to read as speech.

Bell's discovery is one of many that have made speech recognition a reality. Today's speech recognition programs do in fact break down speech into frequencies, as Bell sought to accomplish. They employ many other techniques and information sources as well. Speech recognition programs rely on knowledge about what sounds people make, which differs depending on the language spoken. Japanese, for example, has about 120 possible syllables, while English has more than 10,000. Speech software also incorporates information on sentence structure to help distinguish between words like "to," "too," and "two." NaturallySpeaking and programs like it also learn as you use them. They adapt to the sound of your voice and learn what words and phrases you use most often.

Today's PC has processing power and memory that was just a futuristic dream to early speech researchers. As Dragon Systems co-founder James Baker writes in the foreword to this book, early mainframe computers would take up to an hour to perform the millions of calculations required to recognize a single sentence. Processing power and memory capacity have since shot upwards, while their cost has plummeted. These engineering innovations are essential in making speech recognition practical on your desktop.

How NaturallySpeaking Works

NaturallySpeaking recognizes your speech by using both the sound of your voice and a statistical model of what words tend to go together. Both pieces of information are vital for Naturally-Speaking to achieve acceptable levels of accuracy.

The Sound of Your Voice

As you speak, your vocal folds vibrate and resonate in your chest and throat, creating the unique sound of your voice. This vibration travels through the air like waves moving outward from a stone dropped in a pond. The air vibration reaches your listener's ears, her eardrum vibrates, and her brain interprets this vibration as speech, figuring out your words instantly and unconsciously.

The computer "hears" your voice through a microphone. Microphones have an electrical element sensitive to vibration—an artificial eardrum, in a sense. As the microphone element vibrates, it creates an electrical signal that changes just as fast as your vocal cords vibrated.

The sound card in your computer measures this changing electrical signal, assigning numbers to the signal more than 20,000 times per second. These measurements are so frequent that they give a quite accurate picture of the shape of the electrical changes. This process is called analog-to-digital conversion (Figure 19-1).

Figure 19-1

Analog signal (**A**) is converted to digital (**B** and **C**).

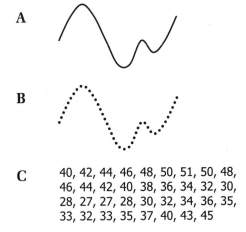

A

B

C

40, 42, 44, 46, 48, 50, 51, 50, 48,
46, 44, 42, 40, 38, 36, 34, 32, 30,
28, 27, 27, 28, 30, 32, 34, 36, 35,
33, 32, 33, 35, 37, 40, 43, 45

The microphone's electrical signal, like the vibration of your speech, is continuous (part **A** in the diagram). The sound card measures the vibration at thousands of points each second. Each measurement is just one moment in time (one dot in **B**), but together they show the shape of the vibration. Each measurement is represented by a number, and the numbers (**C**) are sent to NaturallySpeaking to analyze.

NaturallySpeaking performs many calculations on this stream of numbers as it seeks to determine what you said. The program screens out changes in your voice that aren't useful for recognizing speech. It adjusts the sound signal so that soft words and loud words are treated the same. It also adjusts for the pace of your speech, so that words said rapidly can be recognized by the same methods as words spoken slowly. The software also filters out static and background noise as best it can.

Spoken words are made up of syllables, syllables are made up of short sounds called phonemes, and phonemes are made up of still smaller "sub-phonemic" parts. When you trained NaturallySpeaking to recognize your voice, you allowed the program to model how you, in particular, say all these phonemes and sub-phonemic parts. NaturallySpeaking analyzes the "cleaned-up" numbers from the sound card by comparing them to the basic components of your voice, seeing what speech components match best. The program uses several techniques, including a mathematical tool called Markov Modeling, to seek these key speech components in the sound of your voice. The software then searches for English words that match closely, using a dictionary of tens of thousands of words stored in the computer's active memory (RAM).

Words That Go Together

The sound of your voice is only part of the information NaturallySpeaking uses. Just as important is a statistical model of what words tend to go together. This model allows the program to distinguish between words that sound the same or similar, like "which" and "witch," or "computer is" and "computers." NaturallySpeaking assumes that the words you're saying are grammatical—the word "the" will be followed by a noun, and so on. The software doesn't know actual grammar rules, like following articles by nouns. NaturallySpeaking's "assumptions" were found inductively by analyzing millions of words of English text. The software knows that after you say "the," certain other words are more likely to be said next and other words are not likely to be said next.

NaturallySpeaking combines its calculations on the sound of what you said with its estimates of what words tend to go together. It then generates a list of guesses of what you said, in order of certainty. The program types its best guess on the screen. You can see its other guesses as the alternatives in the Correction window.

Source for information in this section: "When Will HAL Understand What We Are Saying? Computer Speech Recognition and Understanding," by Raymond Kurzweil, in Hal's Legacy, David G. Stork, Editor (Cambridge, MA: The MIT Press, 1997).

Why Are NaturallySpeaking's Mistakes So Funny?

When NaturallySpeaking makes a mistake, it often types out something that's grammatical. Its guesses are not random, as NaturallySpeaking uses statistical models of what words go together in typical English. The software's mistakes thus have the form of regular writing. While reading random words might be dull and perplexing, reading grammatical sentences engages our human intelligence automatically. NaturallySpeaking's bloopers are similar enough to regular writing to provide a context for understanding them, but different enough from real writing to make us howl. It's the old party game "Mad Libs" updated for the computer age! Some examples are provided here for your reading pleasure.

Real-Life Bloopers

▶ I gave the command, "Bring Up Internet Explorer." I was in a rush to go out and just wanted to check one thing. What Dragon typed was "enough internet."

▶ When I try to say "Scratch That" too fast, it types "stress that."
–Judy L., Sherman Oaks, Calif.

▶ When I was writing to one of my penpals I was recovering from a cold. I explained that "I am still sniffing a bit, but at least NaturallySpeaking understands me again." I couldn't have been more wrong…according to the program I was "still sniffing addict." I saw this mistake only *after* I sent the letter.
—Janneke den Draak, The Netherlands

▶ I said, "If you go down to the woods today you're sure of a big surprise." The computer typed, "…you're sure of a big soprano."
—Derek Fawell, U.K.

▶ At the last two Dragon company Christmas parties, a group of us led everyone in singing "The 12 Days of Christmas." We made it a point beforehand to dictate the 12 days of Christmas into different speech recognition engines. If the phrase came out right (rarely) or was boring, we would say it again and again until we got some funny things to say. When you sing them, the words really do sound like the actual lyrics to the song.

12 Robbers Coming
11 Diapers Piping
To Endorse Sleeping (slur the 'to' and 'en-' together)
Vanity Sensing
A Tomato Melting
7 Swanson's Plumbing
Sixties Delaying
5 Golden Rings
4: Birds
3 French Hands
2 Turtle Doubts
and Departure to Repair Tree

—Jeff Foley, Dragon Systems, Newton, Mass.

Send Us Yours

Send us your favorite bloopers! We'll publish the best on our Web site or in a future edition of this book. Bloopers and explanations may be edited for publication. Send bloopers to: Say I Can, 2039 Shattuck Ave. Ste. 500, Berkeley, CA 94704. Or via e-mail to: editor@SayICan.com.

20

Resources

This chapter provides more information on products, resources, and organizations relating to speech recognition and healthy computing.

NaturallySpeaking Accessories

Here a few of the many add-ons that make using NaturallySpeaking faster, easier, and more fun. To learn more about or to purchase products, contact the manufacturer, your local Dragon reseller, or SayICan.com. (See "Where to Buy," page 233.) Because prices change frequently, pricing information is not included here.

Microphones

Headsets (Wired)

Parrott-10
Most users find that this easily adjustable headset mic gives excellent recognition results.

VXI Corporation
One Front Street, P.O. Box 490
Rollinsford, NH 03869

www.vxicorp.com
(603) 742-2888

Andrea ANC-500
This headset includes "active noise cancellation"—circuitry that removes noise from the speech signal. Use this type of microphone to dictate on an airplane, near an air conditioner, or in other high-noise environments.

Andrea Electronics
11-40 45th Road
Long Island City, NY 11101

www.AndreaElectronics.com
(800) 707-5779

Headsets (Wireless)

Wireless microphones free you from being attached to the computer so you can move around as you dictate. Some wireless headsets work by infrared, like a television remote control. Others work by radio signals, which have a wide range but are more subject to interference. Wireless microphone manufacturers include Andrea (see contact information above) and Shure.

Shure Brothers
222 Hartley Avenue
Evanston, IL 60202

www.shure.com
(847) 866-2200

Handheld

Philips SpeechMic
This comfortable handheld microphone includes a trackball and mouse buttons so you can point and click with the same device you use for dictating. You'll especially like this mic if you're used to dictating into a tape recorder with the recorder or microphone close to your mouth.

Philips Speech Processing
64 Perimeter Center East, 6th Floor
P.O. Box 467300
Atlanta, GA 31146

www.speech.be.philips.com
(800) 326-6586

Sennheiser

This company makes expensive (around $500) handheld microphones of excellent quality.

Sennheiser Electronic
One Enterprise Drive
Old Lyme, CT 06371

www.sennheiser.com
(860) 434-9190

Stalk Microphones

These small, stubby microphones work well with portable voice recorders. A stalk model with the same electronics as the VXI Parrott-10 is sold by VXI as the Portable Parrott (see contact information above) and by SRT Distribution.

SRT Distribution
10250 Valley View Road, Suite 143
Eden Prairie, MN 55344

www.srtdist.com
(800) 886-3996

Recorders

Dragon Voice-It

This digital recorder is sold as part of Dragon Naturally-Speaking Mobile, where it's bundled with NaturallySpeaking software. It is also sold separately. This unit has an appealing design and very good recording quality. It also transfers speech files to NaturallySpeaking fairly easily. Achieving best accuracy requires using an external microphone (such as a headset or stalk microphone). Contact Dragon Systems at www.dragonsys.com or Voice-It.

Voice-It Worldwide
2643 Midpoint Drive
Fort Collins, CO 80525

www.voiceit.com
(800) 478-6423

Olympus D1000

The Olympus digital recorder stores your recorded voice on small flash memory cards. The Olympus unit has an excellent built-in microphone and very good recording quality.

Transferring speech files to NaturallySpeaking ranges from easy to difficult depending on your hardware setup.

Olympus America
Two Corporate Center Drive
Melville, NY 11747

www.olympus.com
(800) 622-6372

Norcom and Philips Minicassette Recorders

These devices record on minicassette tapes, which are slightly larger and of higher quality than more familiar microcassettes. All these models are comfortable to use and have good-to-excellent built-in microphones. Recording quality is good, and playing your recorded speech into NaturallySpeaking is simple. The Norcom VoicePort model also functions as a handheld microphone while it's plugged in to the computer. These recorders are good options for people less familiar with computers or who value simplicity.

Philips recorders should be used with the SpeechStar filter, available from SRT Distribution (see contact information above).

Norcom Electronics
30 Lindeman Drive
Trumbull, CT 06611

www.norcom-electronics.com
(203) 374-1500

Sony Minidisc Recorders

Minidiscs have excellent recording quality and can record over two hours on one disk. The MZ-R50 model is appealingly compact but seems designed only for recording and playing music. It is difficult to operate for dictation and has no built-in microphone or speaker. The MZ-B3 model does have an excellent built-in microphone and works well with Naturally-Speaking. However, it's at least twice the size, weight, and price of the other recorders described here.

Sony Electronics
One Sony Drive
Park Ridge, NJ 07676

www.sony.com
(800) 342-5721

Vocabularies

Physicians, attorneys, and law-enforcement personnel can purchase specialized vocabularies to work with NaturallySpeaking. An orthopedist, for example, will typically achieve better accuracy using NaturallySpeaking Professional plus an orthopedic specialty vocabulary than he or she will achieve using NaturallySpeaking Medical Suite, which includes more general medical language. Voice Automated and KorTeam are two leading manufacturers of add-on vocabularies.

Voice Automated   www.voiceautomated.com
215-1/2 Main Street   (800) 597-6600
Huntington Beach, CA 92648

KorTeam International   www.korteam.com
777 Palomar Avenue   (408) 733-7888
Sunnyvale, CA 94086

Macros

KnowBrainer is a different kind of vocabulary add-on. It adds several thousand macros to NaturallySpeaking Professional, Legal, or Medical editions, making it easier to control various parts of Windows and your applications.

Alpha Omega Consulting Group   www.aocg.com
716 Vauxhall Drive   (615) 662-9537
Nashville, TN 37221

The Shortcut Guide On-Screen Reference

The Shortcut Guide to NaturallySpeaking is an on-screen quick reference card that can help you remember and use Naturally-Speaking commands. You press a few keys or say a voice command to display the on-screen help cards. The Shortcut Guide was created from many of the command tables in this book, and it's published by Shortcut Software. For more information or to purchase the guide, visit SayICan.com.

NaturallySpeaking Upgrades

If you registered your software with Dragon Systems, you can upgrade your copy of NaturallySpeaking to a newer version for just a fraction of the cost of buying the whole new version. If you have version 3.52 or below, upgrading will bring significant performance improvements.

You can also upgrade from one edition of NaturallySpeaking to another. You can upgrade, for example, from Preferred to Professional to add macro capability, or from Professional to

Medical to add a medical dictionary. Pricing varies depending on the particular upgrade. For more information, contact Dragon Systems or see "Where to Buy," below.

DragonDictate

DragonDictate, another speech software program made by Dragon Systems, uses older technology that requires you to pause between words. It's useful in four specific cases:

- ▶ If you have a strong accent or speech impairment that NaturallySpeaking does not understand, DragonDictate may still work for you, as it adapts to a wider range of speaking voices.
- ▶ If you work extensively with spreadsheets, the built-in spreadsheet macros in DragonDictate may be useful.
- ▶ If you are a programmer, this software will make working by voice easier with its extensive control of customized vocabularies and complex macros.
- ▶ If you have no hand use at all, use DragonDictate together with NaturallySpeaking to make computing totally hands-free.

Pointing Devices

Cirque Touchpads

This company makes excellent touchpads. They work precisely and require only a light tap on the pad to click.

Cirque   www.cirque.com
433 West Lawndale Drive   (800) 454-3375
Salt Lake City, UT 84115

No-Hands Mouse

This foot-operated mouse has two pedals, one for moving the pointer and one for clicking. It's most practical if you can't use any hand-operated pointing device.

Hunter Digital   www.footmouse.com
11999 San Vicente Blvd.   (800) 576-6873
Suite 400
Los Angeles, CA 90049

Kensington Trackballs

This company's popular trackballs roll easily and have programmable buttons.

Kensington
300 Tower Pkwy.
Lincolnshire, IL 60090

www.kensington.com
(800) 235-6708

Logitech Trackballs

Logitech makes many different pointing devices, including trackballs with a small ball you move with your thumb

Logitech
6505 Kaiser Dr.
Fremont, CA 94555

www.logitech.com
(800) 231-7717

Microsoft EasyBall

This grapefruit-sized trackball, designed for kids, may also be useful to adults with limited hand use.

Microsoft
One Microsoft Way
Redmond, WA 98052

www.microsoft.com
(800) 959-2276

Where to Buy

Your Local Reseller

Some NaturallySpeaking versions are available in software stores everywhere, but other versions are more difficult to come by. Microphones, recorders, and other specialized items are also not widely available. For all these items, contact a Dragon reseller in your area. Your local VAR (for "value-added reseller") can provide you with an informed evaluation of what products are best for your needs. He or she can also provide technical support and personalized training to help you learn the software smoothly. See the Dragon Systems Web site, www.dragonsys.com, for a list of VARs in your area.

SayICan.com

Another source for current products and expert advice is my firm's Web site, SayICan.com. You'll find NaturallySpeaking upgrades, recorders, and other accessories, with helpful reviews and recommendations. The speech recognition world changes much faster than this book can be revised—visit SayICan.com for up-to-date guidance.

NaturallySpeaking and Speech Recognition

Dragon Systems

www.dragonsys.com or www.naturalspeech.com

320 Nevada Street   (800) TALK-TYP or 825-5897 (sales)
Newton, MA 02160   (617) 965-7670 (technical support)

The corporate Web site of Dragon NaturallySpeaking's manufacturer, dragonsys.com hosts a wealth of useful product information. Of particular interest to NaturallySpeaking users is the large, well-organized technical support section. The site lists microphones, sound cards, and computers that Dragon Systems has tested. It also provides contact information for resellers of Dragon products worldwide.

The Unofficial NaturallySpeaking Site

www.synapseadaptive.com/joel/default.htm

This must-read resource is written by Joel Gould, the lead engineer in the creation of NaturallySpeaking 1.0 and 2.0. This insider's guide includes both basic explanations and advanced hacks to make NaturallySpeaking do more things than it's "officially" supposed to. You'll find instructions for changing the NaturallySpeaking default font (which involves editing the Windows registry), a utility called VocEdit that changes the capitalization and spacing of vocabulary words, and much more.

Here's one fun tidbit from the site—an "Easter egg" or hidden feature that's in all versions of NaturallySpeaking. From the NaturallySpeaking Help menu, choose About NaturallySpeaking. Press Shift+F1 and see what appears.

Forums

These Internet discussion groups cover all speech recognition programs. They're a good place to seek advice from other users and exchange technical information.

Voicegroup Discussion Group

www.onelist.com

To subscribe to the Voicegroup e-mail list, visit this Web page and search for "voicegroup."

Voice-Users Discussion Group

www.voicerecognition.com/voice-users

To subscribe to the voice-users e-mail list, enter your e-mail address on this Web page.

For Programmers

ai.iit.nrc.ca/II_public/VoiceCode

This Web site is the home of VoiceGrip, a software tool for programmers working by voice. This site includes links to other programming resources.

Computing Out Loud

www.out-loud.com

This informative site, by long-time speech software user Susan Fulton, contains product reviews, useful tips, and a bloopers page, among other worthwhile resources.

"Fired from the Mouth of My Pet Dragon"

idt.net/~edrose19/page7.html

Written by Ruth Rose, this site contains tips on how to talk to NaturallySpeaking, useful troubleshooting suggestions, and amusing cartoons of dragons.

Repetitive Strain Injury and Disability Information

TIFAQ.com

www.TIFAQ.com

TIFAQ stands for "Typing Injury Frequently Asked Questions." This comprehensive site provides a wealth of information regarding typing injuries and staying healthy. It includes articles, listings, and links to related organizations, reviews of products helpful to people with injuries, and much more. The site is produced by the nonprofit CTD Resource Network (CTD is short for Cumulative Trauma Disorder), which also publishes the newsletter *RSI Network*.

RSI Network

www.ctdrn.org/rsinet.html

This free monthly e-mail newsletter discusses living and working with a repetitive-strain injury. Topics addressed include health improvement techniques and adaptations to working successfully on the computer. To subscribe, visit the web site listed above.

Sorehand Discussion Group

To subscribe to this e-mail discussion group about hand injuries, send e-mail to listserv@itssrv1.ucsf.edu. Include in the body of the message: subscribe sorehand <Firstname> <Lastname>

Association for Repetitive Motion Syndromes (ARMS)

www.certifiedpst.com/arms

P.O. Box 471973
Aurora, CO 80047-1973

This nonprofit membership group advocates on behalf of people with repetitive-strain injuries. It publishes a quarterly newsletter with health tips, medical articles, and listings of repetitive-strain injury support groups everywhere. To join and receive the newsletter, send a $20 check payable to ARMS.

Center for Accessible Technology

www.el.net/CAT

2547 8th Street, #12-A   phone/TTY: (510) 841-3224
Berkeley, CA 94710

This nonprofit center provides information on and guidance in evaluating all types of assistive technology for people with all types of disabilities. CAT staff continually monitor advances in speech recognition and evaluate how it can be used successfully. To join and receive CAT's quarterly newsletter *Real Times*, send a $25 check made payable to CAT.

Closing the Gap

www.closingthegap.com

P.O. Box 68, 526 Main St.   (507) 248-3294
Henderson, MN 56044

This huge online resource includes an easily searchable directory of hardware and software useful for people with disabilities.

Living and Having RSI

This three-page tip sheet reviews how I recovered from my own formerly debilitating repetitive strain injury. Combining physical treatments, lifestyle adjustments, and adaptive equipment and services allowed me to fully regain my health. My most important bit of advice: rest and relax. Read it online in the resources section of SayICan.com.

Your Local RSI Support Group

If you have a repetitive strain injury, exchanging ideas, frustrations, and solutions with people in a similar situation can be vital to improving your health. Local groups typically host physical therapists, adaptive equipment vendors, workers compensation attorneys, and other relevant speakers. They may also have a group library of RSI-related information. Visit the support group in your area, or consider starting a group if none yet exists where you live. For listings of existing support groups, see TIFAQ.com or the ARMS newsletter.

21

Troubleshooting

If NaturallySpeaking is not working as you expect or desire, the suggestions in this chapter can help you sort out what may be going on. When you're troubleshooting problems, restart your computer and load just NaturallySpeaking (if the problem is one you can reproduce in this context). Running NaturallySpeaking by itself simplifies the task of making the program work properly.

The most frequent technical problems are caused by a poor-quality sound system. With a bad sound system, the microphone and sound card combination in the computer provide a signal to NaturallySpeaking that is not clear enough for the software to accurately recognize speech. A second common source of trouble is a conflict between NaturallySpeaking and other programs consuming system resources.

Testing Your Sound System

Test your sound system to see if it gives NaturallySpeaking a clear representation of your voice. You can test using the NaturallySpeaking Audio Setup Wizard in both Automatic and Advanced modes, or test by ear, listening to your recorded speech through your computer's speakers. You've used automatic Audio Setup already, when you first trained NaturallySpeaking to recognize your voice. Using the Advanced mode and testing by ear are necessary only if the automatic Audio Setup Wizard indicates poor sound quality.

Each of these sound testing procedures tests your microphone and sound card in combination. If you have several microphones or sound cards, you can test each combination in turn, but there's no way to test a microphone or sound card independently. Sometimes a microphone model that works well with one sound card will work poorly with another.

Automatic Testing

To test your sound system automatically, choose Audio Setup Wizard from the NaturallySpeaking Tools menu. Follow the on-screen instructions as described in Chapter 2, page 15. The wizard will end with a measurement of sound quality, as in Figure 21-1.

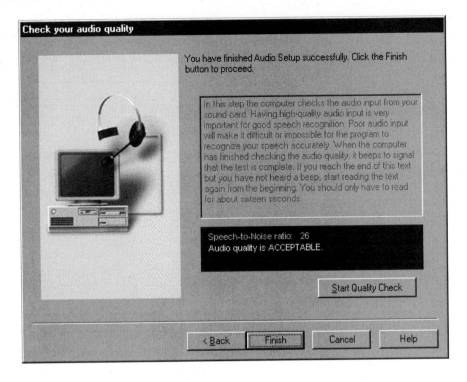

Figure 21-1
These sample test results are for a sound system that's working fine.

Acceptable values for the signal-to-noise ratio range from 15 to 30. If your measured value is below this range, you probably need to change your microphone, sound card, or both.

Advanced Testing

The Audio Setup Wizard has an undocumented Advanced mode which displays sound measurements more precisely. Start by choosing Audio Setup Wizard from the Tools menu. The opening screen appears (Figure 21-2).

Figure 21-2
To use the
Advanced mode,
press Alt+1 from
this screen.

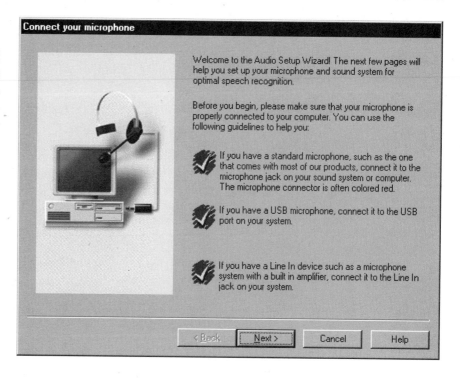

Press Alt+1 (hold down the Alt key and press the "1" key) to switch to Advanced mode (see Figure 21-3).

Figure 21-3
The Advanced
Mode screen. This
example shows a
sound system that's
working well. To
clear measurements
and start a new test,
choose New Test
from the Test menu.

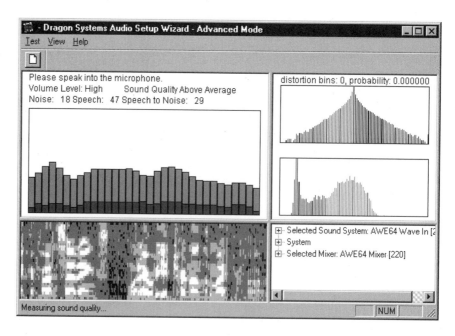

Speak into the microphone for about 30 seconds, until a calculated distortion measurement appears in the upper right corner. For best results, the distortion level should be less than 10. The Advanced Mode window displays measurements of speech, noise, and the speech-to-noise ratio, in decibels. The higher the speech-to-noise ratio, the better your sound system is for speech recognition. The wizard gives a qualitative description of the sound quality, too, based on the speech-to-noise ratio measurement.

Just below the numeric measurements, a bar graph shows signal and noise levels—green bars are speech levels and red bars are noise. Each bar is a different frequency range, from low sounds on the left to high-pitched sounds on the right.

If you're technically inclined, this graph may be helpful in troubleshooting sound problems. For example, I once had a laptop that gave very poor accuracy even with a good microphone. Examining the frequency graph revealed a high speech level but also a very high noise level, with most of the noise in the low frequencies. The poor recognition performance was being caused by a low-frequency noise—in this case, the fan in the laptop. Other common sources of low-frequency noise include defective microphone cables and a power supply or hard drive that generates excessive electrical noise.

In spite of the Audio Setup Wizard's precision measurements, sound system testing has art to it as well as science. Even when the wizard indicates that one microphone has higher sound quality than another, that mic still may perform poorly for a particular user, and a mic that tests poorly in the wizard may still give high accuracy in practical use. For a more detailed discussion of interpreting the Advanced Mode display, see "Reading the Advanced Mode of the Audio Setup Wizard" in the technical support section of www.dragonsys.com.

Testing by Ear

Listening to your car radio, you can probably tell from the clarity of the music and the crackle of static which stations are FM and which are AM without even glancing at the dial. By recording your speech in the computer and playing it back, you can similarly hear whether your voice sounds clear or fuzzy. This can be useful in figuring out what's right or what's wrong with your sound system. Speech that sounds clear and high-fidelity to you will work best for NaturallySpeaking too.

To record and play back, use the sound recorder included with Windows. (This is different from NaturallySpeaking's sound recorder.) From the Windows 98 Start menu, choose Programs, Accessories, Entertainment, Sound Recorder. From the Windows 95 Start menu, choose Programs, Accessories, Multimedia, Sound Recorder. The sound recorder opens (Figure 21-4).

Figure 21-4
The sound recorder.

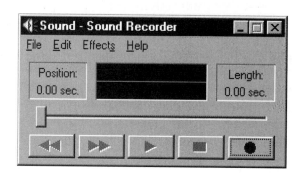

Click the round button once to start recording, then speak into the microphone. Read a sentence, pause silently for a few seconds, and read another sentence, for a total of five to ten seconds of recording. Click the double-left-arrow button to rewind, then the single-right-arrow button to play back.

Adjust the volume of your speakers so that you hear your voice loudly. Ideally, your voice should sound clear and free of static, even when played loudly. In the pause between your sentences, there should be little or no hiss or static.

Figure 21-5
Sound level is set properly.

As your voice is recorded and played back, the green line in the sound recorder should move, creating wave shapes. Ideally, the waves will peak about halfway between the green line and the edge of the box the line is in, as in Figure 21-5.

If the wave forms don't move more than a pixel or two from the green line no matter how loudly you speak (Figure 21-6), or if the wave forms fill the black box completely (Figure 21-7), you need to increase or reduce the volume setting for your sound card.

Figure 21-6
Sound level is too low.

Figure 21-7
Sound level is too high.

To change the volume settings for your sound card, from the Windows 98 Start menu choose Programs, Accessories, Entertainment, Volume Control. From the Windows 95 Start menu, choose Programs, Accessories, Multimedia, Volume Control. A window will appear resembling Figure 21-8. The exact appearance of this window depends on what sound card you have.

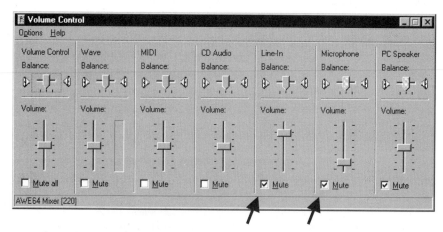

Figure 21-8
Volume controls for
a SoundBlaster card.
Line-in and
Microphone should
be muted, as shown.

The checkboxes below each slider control will say either
Mute or Select, depending on your sound card. If the boxes say
Mute, be sure the boxes below the Line-In and Microphone
sliders are checked (muted). If the boxes say Select, be sure these
two boxes are not checked (not selected).

Next, choose Properties from the Options menu of this
window. The Properties dialog box appears (Figure 21-9).

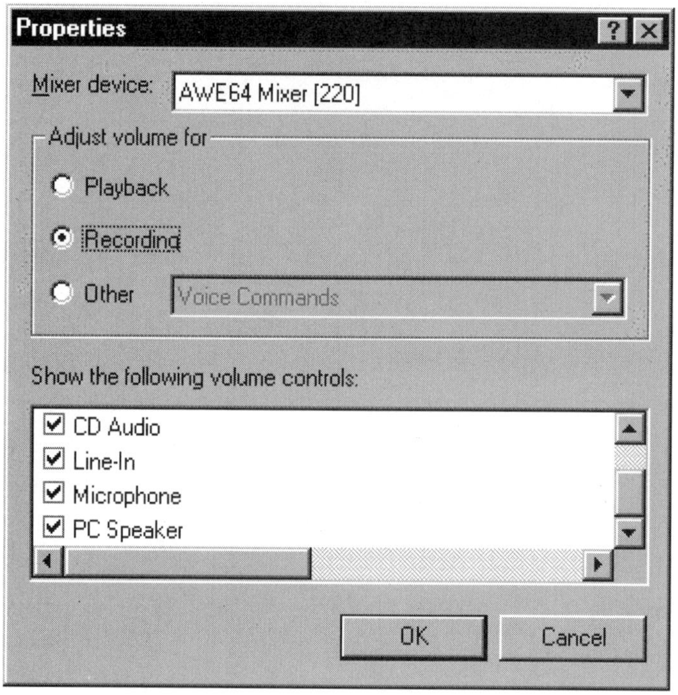

Figure 21-9
Use this dialog box
to display the
recording controls.

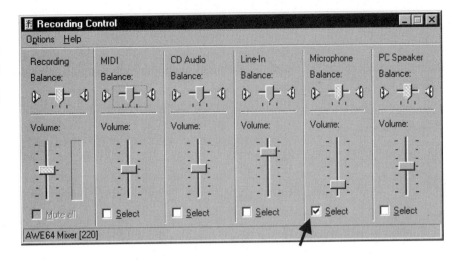

Figure 21-10
The recording
controls. Only
Microphone should
be selected.

Choose Recording. In the lower half of the dialog box, be sure Microphone is checked. Then click OK for the recording controls (Figure 21-10).

If the checkboxes in this window say Select, make sure only the box below the Microphone slider is checked. If the checkboxes say Mute, make sure all boxes are checked (muted) *except* the one below the Microphone slider.

To change the volume level of the signal coming from the sound card, use the mouse to drag the microphone slider up and down. If your voice recorded too softly in the sound recorder (Figure 21-6), drag the slider to the top. If your voice was too loud (Figure 21-7), drag the slider towards the bottom. Leave this recording control window open, switch to the sound recorder, and record another few sentences. Switch back to the recording control window, adjust the microphone slider further, and try recording again.

The Goal

Adjusting the sound system manually lets you determine if your sound system can provide an adequate signal at any setting. In the ideal sound setup, your voice should sound loud and clear when played back from the sound recorder with your speaker volume at normal listening levels. Most computers play a chime sound when Windows starts. To hear your recorded voice in the ideal sound setup, you should not have to turn the volume up to the point where these chimes sound unpleasantly loud. In the ideal sound setup, even if you turn the speaker volume way up, your voice will still sound clear, and no static or hiss will be heard.

In an adequate sound setup, your voice may have a small amount of static, and there may be some background hiss. Still, your voice stands out clearly from any background hiss or static, even with the speakers at normal playback volume. As described above, if the NaturallySpeaking Audio Setup Wizard rates your sound quality as "Acceptable," NaturallySpeaking should work fine.

Fixing Sound Problems

To fix sound problems, try these steps. As you make adjustments, use the NaturallySpeaking Audio Setup Wizard to test sound quality automatically and the Windows Sound Recorder to test quality by ear.

- Review proper microphone positioning (page 13).
- Check that the microphone is plugged into the mic jack on your sound card.
- Disable any voice modem drivers (see below for instructions).
- Disconnect your speakers from the computer, in case they're interfering with the microphone signal.
- Be sure the microphone cable isn't entwined with power cables or other wiring that could cause interference.
- Update your sound card driver to the latest version available. Free updates are usually available from the card manufacturer's Web site.
- Adjust the microphone slider in the recording volume control, as described above (Figure 21-10).
- Try other microphones to see if sound quality improves.
- Try other sound cards to see if sound quality improves.
- If you have a laptop, try unplugging it and operating only on battery power.
- If you have a laptop, try using a USB microphone.

▶ As a last resort, try moving your computer to another location to see if electrical noise in the building wiring is interfering with your sound hardware.

Disabling Voice Modem Drivers

Many modems automatically install a software driver that lets you use the modem similarly to a sound card. To make NaturallySpeaking operate better, disable this driver, which has little practical value anyway. From the Start menu, choose Settings, then Control Panel. Open the System control panel by double-clicking it. Click on the Device Manager tab, then click once on the small plus sign next to the Sound, Video and Game Controllers icon. You'll see a list of all sound drivers installed in your computer (Figure 21-11).

If a driver includes the words "voice" or "voice modem," click on the name once to select it, then click the Properties button. In the dialog box that appears, click Disable in This Hardware Profile and click OK. Click Close to exit the system control panel. The voice modem driver is now disabled.

In the unlikely case that you have more than one sound card installed, the procedure just described should be used to disable the sound card you prefer not to use.

Figure 21-11
A voice modem driver is highlighted in the system shown.

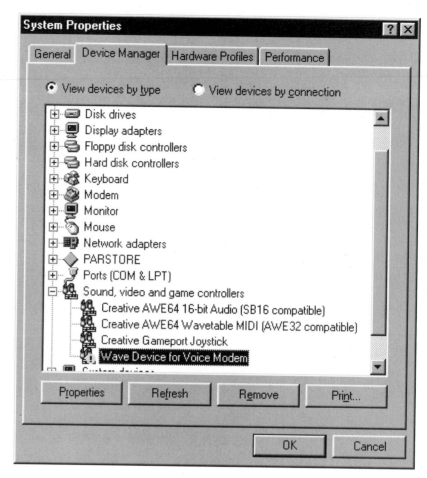

Software Conflicts

Conflicts with other software programs can cause system errors, freezes, and crashes. Conflicts with other programs competing for system resources can also cause NaturallySpeaking to perform slowly or inaccurately. For the fastest, most reliable performance, avoid having other programs run in the background while using NaturallySpeaking. Programs that run in the background compete with NaturallySpeaking for computing power and memory access, slowing performance and increasing the chance of a crash or software error.

Determining What Programs Run in the Background

To see what programs automatically operate in the background on your computer, restart your computer and wait for Windows to finish loading. Looking at the Windows desktop, and before opening any programs, hold down the Ctrl and Alt keys and tap the Delete key. The Close Program dialog box appears (Figure 21-12).

Figure 21-12
Display this window before starting any programs. In the ideal system, only Explorer and Systray will be listed.

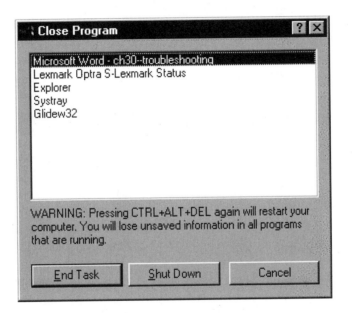

This dialog box shows all the programs running on your computer at the moment. For fastest and most reliable Naturally-Speaking performance, only Explorer and Systray should be listed in this window when Windows first starts. If your computer is like most, there will be anywhere from two to ten other items listed. These programs might include antivirus software, special drivers for a mouse or joystick, and scheduling programs for backup, financial, and contact management software. Often it's not obvious what each program is from its name.

To reduce software conflicts and improve NaturallySpeaking's performance, you need to prevent all of these programs from loading when your computer starts. This may involve a tradeoff of convenience. Removing a scheduling program will prevent appointment alarms (from, for example, ACT! or

GoldMine) from appearing. Turning off antivirus software leaves your computer more open to virus trouble. You may choose to keep these and the other programs that start automatically.

Not all programs cause problems. The more programs running in the background, the more chance of slowdowns and crashes, but there is no certainty to it. If NaturallySpeaking is working fine, leave your computer be. If you experience slow performance and crashes, remove every background program except the ones you really need. On my computer, for example, I leave software for my touchpad installed and NaturallySpeaking still works fine. However, I run my computer without the bill-reminder feature in Quicken and without the Microsoft Office Fast Find feature and Office Toolbar, as these are software components I can live without.

Preventing Background Programs from Loading

To stop most programs from loading automatically, delete the shortcut to that program present in the Windows StartUp folder. Find these programs by choosing Find... Files or Folders from the Windows Start menu. Type "startup" as the name to search for and have the computer search on your main hard disk drive (usually drive C:) as in Figure 21-13.

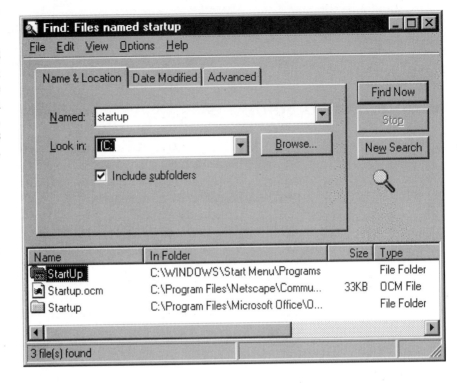

Figure 21-13
Files and folders on
the main hard drive
named "startup." In
the system shown,
the desired folder is
the first in the list.

The most common path for the StartUp folder:

C:\Windows\Start Menu\Programs\StartUp

Double-click on the StartUp folder to open it. Move all files
in this folder to a new folder on your desktop (call it "Unused
Startup Items"). If you choose to reinstall these startup items,
just move them back to the StartUp folder, their original location.

With the StartUp folder now empty, restart the computer and
open the Close Program dialog box once again (press
Ctrl+Alt+Delete). If you see only Explorer and Systray, you have
successfully removed all background programs that run
automatically. If programs besides Explorer and Systray still
remain, you'll need to try several different approaches to remove
them. Some programs have an options setting that lets you turn
off features that load automatically. The Billminder feature in
some versions of Quicken is like this, and antivirus software also
works this way. In some cases you'll need to uninstall a program
completely to prevent it from loading automatically.

To prevent software from automatically loading, begin by removing all items from the StartUp menu, as described. Continue to more involved techniques only if NaturallySpeaking still does not operate correctly.

Problems and Solutions

Here are common problems users encounter, along with suggested solutions.

No Response when Dictating

Symptom: You've previously been dictating successfully, but now when you speak into the microphone there's no response.

Possible Causes and Solutions: Check that the microphone is plugged in to the correct jack on the sound card. Check that the microphone is turned on in NaturallySpeaking and not in sleep mode. Check that the window you want to dictate to is active. To make a window active, click once on it's title bar. To check that a window is active and can receive dictation, type a few characters on the keyboard and make sure they show up on screen.

Word and WordPerfect

In Word and WordPerfect, you can increase performance and reduce the chance of problems by turning off features that act as you type, such as automatic spelling and grammar checking and features that automatically expand abbreviations.

Symptom: No NaturalWord menu appears—the menus in your Word or WordPerfect program do not include one named Dragon NaturallySpeaking. Properly installed, this menu is typically just to the right of the Help menu.

Cause: The NaturalWord link is not installed.

Solution: Restart your computer. After Windows starts, insert the NaturallySpeaking CD-ROM and follow the instructions to begin installation. Install the NaturalWord link to your word processor by checking only that one checkbox in the installation program (uncheck the other boxes).

If the NaturalWord link to your word processor does not appear as an installation option, NaturallySpeaking cannot find your word processor to install the link. Be sure your word processor is Word 97, Word 2000, WordPerfect 8, or WordPerfect 9, and if it is, contact Dragon technical support for instructions on how to install the link without using the main Naturally-Speaking installation program.

Symptom: Natural Language commands don't work, or you can't select text by voice.

Solution: This problem has the same cause and solution as the symptom above. Natural Language commands are available in Word 97 and Word 2000 only.

Internet Explorer

Symptom: Can't say links or otherwise control Internet Explorer by voice.

Possible Causes and Solutions: NaturallySpeaking must be started before Internet Explorer. Alternately, you may need to change an option in Internet Explorer that lets the program communicate with NaturallySpeaking. From the View menu in Internet Explorer, choose Internet Options and click on the Advanced tab. Make sure the "Browse in a new process" box is checked (Internet Explorer 4.0) or the "Launch browser windows in separate process" box is checked (if you have version 5.0).

Commands

Symptom: Commands are often typed as text.

Possible Cause: NaturallySpeaking expects no pauses between the words in the command.

Solution: Run the words in the command together so there are no pauses in the middle. If this doesn't work, increase the Pause Between Phrases value in NaturallySpeaking's Options (see page 216).

Symptom: Commands said after dictation are sometimes typed as text.

Possible Cause: NaturallySpeaking expects a longer pause between dictation and the command.

Solution: Pause for a longer time before saying the command. If this doesn't work or is awkward, make the "Pause Between Phrases" setting shorter in NaturallySpeaking's Options (see page 216).

Symptom: One or more specific commands are always typed as text.

Possible Causes and Solutions: Try saying the command while holding down the Ctrl key. If the command still doesn't work, this command is not available in the application you're using. If the command does work with the Ctrl key held down, retrain the command so the computer will recognize it more accurately (see page 175).

Symptom: You can't select text by voice.

Cause: Your application is not Select-and-Say.

Solution: If you're using Word or WordPerfect, activate the NaturalWord link (see "Word and WordPerfect" troubleshooting section above). Otherwise, there is no solution—you can only select by voice in Select-and-Say applications.

Symptom: You can't spell numbers or special characters in the Correction window.

Cause: Your voice files were upgraded from an older NaturallySpeaking version to version 4 and upgrading the files this way does not add the new version 4 commands.

Solution: Create a new user and train from the beginning. This is the only way to add the new version 4 commands.

Very Low Accuracy

Symptom: NaturallySpeaking's accuracy is very low (less than about 80%).

Causes: This might be due to other programs competing with NaturallySpeaking for system resources. Or, your sound signal may be very noisy.

Try these steps:

- ▶ Be sure that the microphone element is pointed towards your mouth (take off the windscreen to check).
- ▶ Reduce or eliminate background noise.
- ▶ See "Testing Your Sound System" above to check your microphone and sound card.
- ▶ See "Software Conflicts" above to remove other programs competing for system resources.

Added Words

Symptom: NaturallySpeaking types words that you didn't say, even when you're not speaking.

Cause: The program is hearing sounds that it interprets as words.

Try these steps:

▶ Move the microphone toward the corner of your mouth.
▶ If the microphone is already at the corner of your mouth, move it further away (outward) from your mouth.
▶ Clip the microphone cord to your shirt or tuck it in your belt so it doesn't rustle against your clothes.
▶ Reduce background noise.
▶ Check that your sound system is not introducing static. See "Testing Your Sound System" above. If you have a laptop, test it when operating from batteries only as well as from the wall outlet.

Slow Performance

Symptom: There's a long pause between when you dictate your first sentence in a NaturallySpeaking session and when the sentence appears on screen. There's also a long pause (five to ten seconds) after choosing the correct word or phrase in the Correction window.

Causes and Solutions: If you have 64 MB of RAM or less, adding more memory will probably eliminate these delays. The pauses might also be due to other programs competing with NaturallySpeaking for system resources. See "Software Conflicts" above. This behavior is normal for Pentium 166-MHz and slower processors.

Symptom: NaturallySpeaking performance is very slow in general. The computer lags far behind your dictation. Accuracy may also be very low (less than 80%).

Causes and Solutions: This might be due to other programs competing with NaturallySpeaking for system resources. See "Software Conflicts" above. Or, your sound signal may be very noisy, so NaturallySpeaking must spend processing time filtering the noise.

Try these steps:

▶ Be sure that the microphone element is pointed towards your mouth (take off the windscreen to check).
▶ Reduce or eliminate background noise.
▶ See "Testing Your Sound System" above to check your microphone and sound card.
▶ See "Software Conflicts" above to remove other programs competing for system resources.

Recorded Speech Playback

To make recorded speech playback work better, you can change the amount of audio NaturallySpeaking records. From the Tools menu in the NaturallySpeaking window, choose Options, then the Miscellaneous tab. Change the Disk Space Reserved for Speech Data value to a higher number—perhaps 60 or 80 MB. Unfortunately, this change does not usually have much effect. Note also that recorded speech is not available in Naturally-Speaking Standard Edition.

If recorded speech is routinely unavailable during the first section of a long stretch of dictation but available during the last part of the dictation, you may be able to fix this problem using the advanced technique of editing the Windows registry. See the technical support section of the Dragon Systems Web site (www.dragonsys.com) for instructions.

Macro Troubleshooting

This section describes common reasons why macros do not work and how to fix them. To use a macro, say the macro name. Remember to pause before and after saying it. The computer will execute the macro—it will type the text or run the script you associated with that macro name. If a macro does not work properly, it's due to one of these two reasons:

▶ NaturallySpeaking does not recognize the macro name.
▶ NaturallySpeaking recognizes the macro name and executes it, but the macro does not do what you want it to do.

A useful technique in diagnosing macro problems is to hold down the Ctrl key while saying the macro name. This forces NaturallySpeaking to recognize only commands and macros, not dictation words.

Global Macros

Follow these steps when troubleshooting a global macro—one that should work in all applications. Which of these three things happens when you say the macro name?

> (1) NaturallySpeaking types the macro name—it doesn't actually execute the macro.
> (2) NaturallySpeaking types words that are different from the macro name.
> (3) NaturallySpeaking types nothing. However, the macro name does appear in the Results box. The Results box is the small yellow box that appears while you dictate. It looks like this: `business address`

▶ If (1) occurs—NaturallySpeaking types the macro name— hold down the Ctrl key and say the macro name again. What happens?

> ▶ (1a): It works—the macro executes. This indicates that NaturallySpeaking is confusing the macro name with another word or phrase. To fix this problem, change the macro name to a name distinct from other words and phrases. Try making the name longer, using longer words in the name, or both.
>
> ▶ (1b): Nothing happens. This indicates that the macro is not available in the application you're in. The most likely causes are that the macro was created as application-specific instead of global, or the macro was not saved. To determine what happened, choose Edit Command Wizard, select Global, and look for the macro name in the list of all global commands. It won't be there. The fix is to create the macro again using the New Command Wizard. Make sure to choose Global on the first screen (Figure 11-1, page 107).

▶ If (2) occurs—NaturallySpeaking types words that are different from the macro name—hold down the Ctrl key and say the macro name again. What happens?

▶ (2a): It works—the macro executes. This indicates that the macro is set up fine but is not being recognized correctly. To fix this, train the macro (Tools menu, Train) and try again. If it still does not work, change the macro name to be more distinct from other words and phrases. Try making the name longer, using longer words in the name, or both.

▶ (2b): Nothing happens. This indicates that the macro is not available in the application you're in. The most likely causes are that the macro was created as application-specific instead of global, or the macro was not saved. To determine what happened, choose Edit Command Wizard, select Global, and look for the macro name in the list of all global commands. It won't be there. To fix it, create the macro again using the New Command Wizard. Make sure to choose Global on the first screen (Figure 11-1, page 107).

▶ If (3) occurs—NaturallySpeaking types nothing—this indicates that NaturallySpeaking is recognizing and executing the macro correctly. Here are three possible causes of the problem:

▶ The macro's author made a mistake in specifying what the macro should do. For example, the macro may have been accidentally set to type nothing. Or, the macro enters keystrokes that do nothing or runs a script that doesn't have any effect. The fix is to edit the text or script this macro is supposed to type or execute.

▶ The program, window, or dialog box that's active when you say the macro doesn't accept the keystrokes the macro sends. For example, in the program Paint, saying "business address" will have no effect. Paint is a graphics program, and typing text has no effect on it. The fix: Don't use the macro with this program or window.

▶ A bug in NaturallySpeaking is causing the error. If your macro just types keystrokes, a bug is probably not the source of your problem. If your macro executes script commands, however, such as HeardWord, the problem may be due to a NaturallySpeaking programming error.

Try rewriting the macro using different script commands to achieve the same result.

Application-Specific Macros

Follow these steps when troubleshooting an application-specific macro—one that's meant to work only in one application. Which of these three things happens when you say the macro name?

(1) NaturallySpeaking types the macro name—it doesn't actually execute the macro.

(2) NaturallySpeaking types words that are different from the macro name.

(3) NaturallySpeaking types nothing. However, the macro name does appear in the Results box. The Results box is the small yellow box that appears while you dictate. It looks like this: business address

▶ If (1) occurs—NaturallySpeaking types the macro name—hold down the Ctrl key and say the macro name again. What happens?

   ▶ (1a): It works—the macro executes. This indicates that NaturallySpeaking is confusing the macro name with another word or phrase. To fix this problem, change the macro name to a name distinct from other words and phrases. Try making the name longer, using longer words in the name, or both.

   ▶ (1b): Nothing happens. This indicates that the macro is not available in the application you're in. Likely causes are that the macro was not saved, was created in the wrong application, or was created in the right application but under the wrong window name. To fix this problem, create the macro again using the New Command Wizard. Create it under a different window name than the first time if there are several window names to choose from.

▶ If (2) occurs—NaturallySpeaking types words that are different from the macro name—hold down the Ctrl key and say the macro name again. What happens?

▶ (2a): It works—the macro executes. This indicates that the macro is set up fine but is not being recognized correctly. To fix this, train the macro (Tools menu, Train) and try again. If it still does not work, change the macro name to be more distinct from other words and phrases. Try making the name longer, using longer words in the name, or both.

▶ (2b): Nothing happens. This indicates that the macro is not available in the application you're in. The most likely causes are that the macro was not saved, was created in the wrong application, or was created in the right application but under the wrong window name. To fix it, create the macro again using New Command Wizard. Create it under a different window name than the first time if there are several window names to choose from.

▶ If (3) occurs—NaturallySpeaking types nothing—this indicates that NaturallySpeaking is recognizing and executing the macro correctly. Here are three possible causes of the problem:

▶ The macro's author made a mistake in specifying what the macro should do. For example, the macro may have been accidentally set to type nothing. Or, the macro enters keystrokes that do nothing or runs a script that doesn't have any effect. The fix is to edit the text or script this macro is supposed to type or execute.

▶ The program, window, or dialog box that's active when you say the macro doesn't accept the keystrokes the macro sends. For example, in the program Paint, saying "business address" will have no effect. Paint is a graphics program, and typing text has no effect on it. The fix: Don't use the macro with this program or window.

▶ A bug in NaturallySpeaking is causing the error. If your macro just types keystrokes, a bug is probably not the source of your problem. If your macro executes script commands, however, such as HeardWord, the problem may be due to a NaturallySpeaking programming error. Try rewriting the macro using different script commands to achieve the desired result.

Index

Feedback

Help us improve this book. If you think of a way to make the next edition better, please send it along. Please note that we are unable to answer technical inquiries. Send suggestions to editor@SayICan.com, or fax to (510) 644-9436.

Also from Waveside Publishing

Book Order Form

....

Phone	Call Toll-Free, 1 **(877) SAY-I-CAN** or 1 (877) 729-4226
Web	Visit **SayICan.com**
Fax	Fax orders to (510) 644-9436
Mail	Say I Can, 2039 Shattuck Ave. Ste. 500 Berkeley, CA 94704

Please send:

_____ *copies of* Talk to Your Computer ($14.95 each)
_____ *copies of* The Dragon NaturallySpeaking Guide ($19.95 each)

Your satisfaction guaranteed or return within 90 days for a full refund (excluding shipping).

Name: _____

Address: _____

City: _____ State: _____ Zip: _____

Phone: (____) _____

Sales Tax
California mailing addresses: please add 8.25% for Alameda County, 7.25% for other California counties.

Shipping
$3.95 for first book, $0.80 each additional book.
Outside U.S.: $11 for first book, $5 each additional book (estimate)

Payment
[ ] VISA [ ] MasterCard [ ] Amex   [ ] Check enclosed
                                          payable to Say I Can

Card number: _____

Name on card: _____ Exp. Date: _____

Quantity discounts available for purchases of 10 books or more—for details, order by phone or visit **SayICan.com**. Prices subject to change.